Fairy Tales in Psychotherapy

Table of Contents

PART III: ADVANTAGES OF USING FAIRY TALES IN PSYCHOTHERAPY

Fairy Tales in Psychotherapy

The Creative Use of Old and New Tales

by

Erich Franzke

Translated from the German by
Joseph A. Smith

Hogrefe & Huber Publishers
Toronto • Lewiston, NY • Bern • Göttingen

This work is a licensed translation of
MÄRCHEN AND MÄRCHENSPIEL IN DER PSYCHOTHERAPIE:
DER KREATIVE UMGANG MIT ALTEN UND NEUEN GESCHICHTEN
Copyright 1985 by Verlag Hans Huber, Bern • Stuttgart • Toronto

The figures mentioned in the text have been placed on eight pages in the middle of the book; the color figures are numbered in Roman, the black-and-white figures in Arabic numerals. The author and publisher thank Mr. Anders Roos for allowing them to reprint the picture of the Sleeping Beauty castle. The titles of the fairy tales of the Grimm Brothers quoted in this volume follow, for the most part, those of a translation published in 1812. The translations of the texts are by the translator.

Library of Congress Cataloging-in-Publication Data

Franzke, Erich.
[Märchen und Märchenspiel in der Psychotherapie. English]
Fairy tales in psychotherapy : the creative use of old and new stories / Erich Franzke : translated from the German by Joseph A. Smith
p. cm.
Translation of: Märchen and Märchenspiel in der Psychotherapie : der kreative Umgang mit alten und neuen Geschichten.
Bibliography: p.
Includes index.
1. Fairy tales—Psychological aspects. 2. Fairy tales—Therapeutic use. 3. Psychotherapy. I. Title.
RC489.F3F7313   1989   616.89'14—dc 18   88-22059

Canadian Cataloguing in Publication Data

Franzke, Erich, 1927–
Fairy tales in psychotherapy
Translation of: Märchen and Märchenspiel in der Psychotherapie
Bibliography: p.
Includes index.
1. Psychotherapy. Fairy tales—Therapeutic use. 2. Play therapy. I. Title.
RC489.F3F713   1989   616.89'16   C88-094490-0

Printed in the United States of America

ISBN 0-920887-42-2 Hans Huber Publishers • Toronto • Lewiston, NY • Bern • Stuttgart
ISBN 3-456-81725-8 Hans Huber Publishers • Bern • Stuttgart • Toronto • Lewiston, NY

Only criteria important for practical psychotherapeutic work are discussed here. The term *fairy tale* is to be understood broadly. The following criteria were deemed necessary to warrant inclusion:

- The crossing of limits otherwise set by reality, whereby it is of no importance whether we are dealing with large, fantastic, magical, even "godlike" capabilities, or whether only slight details signal the transition to the realm of "surplus reality."*

- The presence of metamorphic phenomena and/or stages of development and growth. The spectrum ranges from small changes to dying and becoming.

- The use of allegory, illustrations, examples (as carriers of meaning), in order to illuminate parallel processes in the client and his/her situation, both now and in the past.

- Being moved by the fairy-tale content—the stirring of our deepest feelings, beyond ratio and reason, in the realm of our mental *images*.

- Long and intensive experience with the work methods shown.

Folk, Family, Children's, and Maturation Tales

Here, one could emphasize several very different aspects [28, pp. 10–11]. We are interested particularly in therapeutic viewpoints. Various schools of psychology

---

* In the depiction of real events in psychodrama, Moreno [39] speaks of "semi-reality," whereas he views role-playing with its "impossible," future, fairy-tale-like, mythical, fantastic contents as being in the realm of "surplus reality"—which permits an extension of consciousness; cf. Leutz [36], pp. 119–140.

have treated the theme of fairy tales in the past [13, 14, 17, 27]. I would like to point out a few things that are important to the practical work in this area:

- The written form was recorded only after a very long oral tradition, whereby the general context was more or less changed, "refined," or, in some cases, even weakened.

- The language used is graphic, decidedly simple, and missing some details. This gives space for individual variations. Everyone can (re)discover personal meanings, ideas, and associations according to own experience. And because of the short and succinct descriptions and the simple characters in such tales, generally valid and encompassing contents and functions become clear.

- Many fairy tales were not originally intended for children, but rather were stories told in the spinning-room. They allowed the older, more experienced women to pass on wisdoms in an allegorical, symbolic form to the younger women—who were often also working at the very time on their dowry.

- Some recurring themes are dealt with in very diverse forms, not only in various cultures, but also from story to story, sometimes with very different results. Verena Kast [28, 29] has treated some of these themes. This is discussed in the later section covering the different work methods (p. 67), since it plays a role in the selection of appropriate fairy tales for psychotherapeutic purposes.

- Dieckmann [6, 7] studied the connections with the personal life history and situation.

Sagas, Legends, Myths, Allegories, Fables, Children's Songs, and Folksongs

I do not draw a sharp lines between these genres, nor do I attempt exact definitions. This is not for reasons of space. Rather, in this work the *therapeutic utility* is of major importance as well as the presentation of work methods and selection criteria. The (incomplete) listing above serves only to stimulate thought and to avoid reducing matters to "fairy tales and nothing else." "What is a fairy tale, a saga, etc., and what is not?" is a matter of less importance for therapy and is thus not treated here.

Verena Kast presents in one of her books, *Paare* (Couples) [30], the links and parallels of myths to the life situation and fantasies of human beings. Examples of the use of children's stories and folksongs may be found in this book as well (see pages 23 and 107). The "epic" of *Philipp and Eberhard* created by course participants (pages 37 and 85) is most certainly not a fairy tale. But it will be left up to the readers to judge this at the appropriate time and in accordance with their own feelings.

Fairy Tales, Myths, Sagas, etc., from Foreign Cultures

My 25 years of work in Sweden have brought me into contact with Scandinavian sagas and fairy tales not only intellectually, but also by direct experience through my own children. My involvement began with children's songs and rhymes, which are psychodynamically also of great interest. Even the melodies are very different. Songs in minor keys are found more often in Scandinavian children's songs than in those of Middle Europe. Non-Scandinavians often interpret this to denote sadness or resignation, missing the warmth and depth. But songs in minor keys fit very well the various meetings with elves, trolls [49], and "skogsrån" (beautiful and bewitching cow-tailed "forest women" with a function similar to the Loreley) found in many Scandinavian tales. In time these songs unfolded for me— though I cannot clearly define the difference in feeling I have between them and Middle European ones. To attempt this rationally causes some of the essence to be lost.

An example: The "valse triste" by Jean Sibelius, interpreted by a good Middle or Southern European orchestra, often loses its deep melancholic warmth and expresses solely a heavy pathos. Exactly played, however, it has a considerably different feeling: The difference between "well played" and "letting it flow" is very big indeed. Someone who has spent some time in the Scandinavian countries can, for example, hear the Scandinavian influence of Smetana's years in Göteborg in the river motif of his Moldau.

Through these experiences I became especially interested in the use of foreign fairy tales (in the broad sense). At international conferences one could observe time and again how exciting and deep the confrontation was with fairy tales, myths, and sagas of other countries and continents. Both participants and therapists are more open to individual interpretations—and further removed from cliches—when working with foreign material. After hearing a foreign fairy tale or seeing a stage presentation thereof, the following questions often arise: "What else can that mean?" — "What is different in our tales?" — "What is apparently valid for all humans, and what are the variations on these general themes?" This more or less automatic reaction to such "foreignness" can, in therapy, actually help to reveal and pinpoint the relevance of fairy tales to the *particular individual*. (See page 80 for a practical example of this.)

Literary Fairy Tales

This term denotes, without respect of the actual artistic quality, all fairy tales, animal stories, fables, children's stories, etc., that have a single author and that are available to the general public.

For practical therapeutic reasons, it is important that these forms be differentiated from the traditional, oral types. Here, the content and the form reflect upon the author; his or her feelings, interests, and objectives, inasmuch as they appear, must be reckoned with. This may even cause a particular author to become one's personal "favorite." The subtle fairy tales and animal stories of Manfred Kyber [33, 34], for example, attract other readers than, say, the often tragic tales of Hans Christian Andersen [1]. In the latter, a happy end is reached only after severe trials, or only on a "higher level"—if at all. In the autobiographical introduction to his collected fairy tales entitled "The Tale of My Life. Without Poetic Enhancement," Andersen expressly mentions that in certain tales he describes some important persons from his own life.

When special capabilities are described, for example, in Astrid Lindgren's *Pippi Longstocking* series [37], one should not draw one-sided conclusions about the personality of a (young) reader excited by the story. Instead of simply assuming that the person has tendencies to overestimate his or her abilities, one should consider illusionary, passive overblown expectations or (over)compensating elements as well. It should at least be asked whether the reader is taking on the role described, admires the capabilities in question, or wishes to meet someone similar in order to receive help. But these are not the only possibilities: In some fables the educational, moral, or straightforwardly moralizing character is so clearly primary that they are better suited to guiding the reader than to serving as examples of multi-layered, complicated states of mind. An example of this is the story of *Struwwelpeter* (Tousle-Haired Peter) by Heinrich Hoffmann [25], who by the way was a physician.

It should also be mentioned that not so much the content as the emotional relationship between the storyteller and the listener is decisive in whether and to what extent such a story serves to further or stunt development. By this I mean that the diagnostic value of a client's preference for one author over another can be high indeed; hard and fast ideologies of a client can often be reached more readily through this roundabout way than by attacking the problem directly. Except for the differences noted, the same possibilities are available when using literary tales as with traditional ones.

Personal Fairy Tales

A very widely practiced form of this genre are the fairy tales and bedtime stories parents think up specially for their children. Here, too, of course, we meet with all sorts, from the subtlest tales meant to deepen the contact between child and parent, to hair-raising horror stories as educational measures. Such stories often tell us more about the *author* than about the listener. Here again, the basic emotional relationship between storyteller and listener is decisive to the reaction of the latter.

For practical purposes, one differentiates between family fairy tales, individual fairy tales, and utility tales. In the first, social factors play a large role; these tales are relevant on the object level. With individual fairy tales, intrapsychic events are of primary interest; they further our understanding of the subject level. In utility tales, finally, educational and other objectives are primary. Often all three facets may be found in a single story. The following personal fairy tale of a nearly 50-year-old female participant of a seminar in continuing education may serve as an example of such overlapping. Some points of particular importance to an understanding of the author will be discussed later.

Belle Rose

Once upon a time there was a lonely house at the shore where lived a father, a mother, and their small son, Peter. The father worked the lighthouse and watched over the channel that flowed inland; the mother worked in the house and took care of the garden. Peter was often alone, and he complained that he had neither playmates nor brothers and sisters. One rainy day Peter was playing in the attic, going through old boxes and crates. There he discovered in an old dusty trunk an equally old gray doll whose faded clothes were nearly falling off. Peter lifted the doll up carefully; the doll's eyelids in the pale porcelain face remained closed. Peter then brought the doll to his mother, who gazed upon it with astonishment, for she recognized her own old doll "Belle Rose" which her grandfather had brought her many years ago from one of his trips in foreign lands. She remembered that the grandfather had said that the doll could come to life. Since Peter wanted to play with the old doll, the mother took off the old clothes, washed the face and body, and that evening while Peter was asleep sewed a new dress of a beautiful sky-blue color.

The father did not approve of Peter's playing with dolls. But because the mother beseeched him to allow the boy to have his fun, the father finally agreed. And when the mother laid Belle Rose next to Peter in his bed, she had the feeling that the doll's cheeks were somewhat redder, and that the mouth had opened slightly. The eyes, which opened now with a soft click when the doll was picked up, were radiant blue like Peter's.

Peter played every day with Belle Rose. He took the doll with him wherever he went, and it became a part of his life. The father built a small wooden wagon for Belle Rose. And every evening, when Peter's parents came to say goodnight, they also had to wish Belle Rose a goodnight, and soon both slept soundly. So it was until Spring came, when one day great noise and bustle was heard from outside. As every year, the workers with their families had come to work on the channel. They arrived with their many children, caravans, and tents, and even a German shepherd dog was there. Peter was happy finally to have playmates once again, though he had learned in the meantime that they would all leave after a few weeks. Suddenly he felt ashamed playing with a doll in front of the other boys and left Belle Rose in the house. A few days later Peter noticed one morning that Belle Rose looked pale and sad. Peter's heart sank. He placed Belle Rose in the wooden wagon and set her in front of the house in the sun. With a sense of relief, he then ran off and played with the other children.

The German shepherd, still young and frisky, tried over and again to catch the ball, so that finally the children chased him away. The dog roamed around seeking a new pastime, whereupon he discovered Belle Rose sitting in the wagon; she smelled so much like a human being. Carefully he took Belle Rose between his teeth and ran off with her. When he came by the children, they all laughed and called out that he was carrying a doll in his mouth. Peter looked up and saw that it was Belle Rose dangling helplessly back and forth from the dog's mouth. He screamed and ran after the dog, who with a start ran toward the channel. The other children ran screaming and laughing after them and made fun of Peter that he had become so excited over an old doll. The dog was so upset by the loud noise that he let the doll fall and ran away. Belle Rose then rolled down the embankment and fell into the water. Peter froze, then he slid more than ran after her and tried to reach her from the bank, but without success. Peter went into the water and sank immediately, since the channel was very deep. As he came up again, he lurched at Belle Rose, who had already been driven further by the rushing waters. The children on the bank screamed now out of fear and despair, as they watched Peter go under water again and again.

Finally, some grown-ups came, among them Peter's father, who immediately saw the danger and jumped into the water. He grabbed Peter by his blond hair and pulled him up out of the water. Peter, who was by now nearly unconscious, held Belle Rose tightly in his arms. The father swam to the bank where some men pulled them up. Then he brought Peter home and gave him to the terrified mother. The father, still trembling from the fear he had felt for his son, railed that he'd risked his life because of some dumb old doll. The mother briskly dried Peter off who was slowly coming to and beginning to chill. Afterwards she laid him in his bed and covered him up warmly. Peter held the still-wet doll so tightly in his arms that the mother could not free her. So she wrapped up the both of them in blankets. For a moment she had the feeling that Belle Rose was suddenly much larger, that her cheeks and lips were redder than before. That night Peter developed a fever, and he dreamed that a small warm child was lying next to him. When the mother came to his bed in the morning, she couldn't believe her eyes: Beside Peter, who slept soundly, slept a healthy little girl—Belle Rose. The mother ran out and got the father, and he too could not believe the miracle that had happened. Then it occurred to the mother what her grandfather had said about Belle Rose coming to life if someone were to really love her. And the four of them lived happily ever after.

The story of Belle Rose (I won't discuss the meaning of the name any further here) occurred to the woman after I had, at the end of the first group session, mentioned that old or new stories of the participants were welcome. She had thought up the story of Belle Rose originally for her small children many years ago when she herself lay in bed with fever and couldn't play. On the subject of the rediscovered doll, she recalled that she too had received her favorite doll from her beloved grandfather.

Without going further into "Hoffmann's Tales" or the story of Pinocchio, one should remark shortly upon the theme of a doll recovered from an old trunk coming to life. Later, Peter again "forgot" the doll upon finding playmates with whom he could carry out masculine activities; Belle Rose had to be nearly lost before Peter regained his interest in her. The storyteller herself had been overworked and overburdened for many years, through her job, through her duties as a mother, and at times through her nearly complete responsibility for the entire family. Neither the time nor the energy could be spared for her own desires and creative interests. The little girl in her—the sensitive and emotional woman—had to take a back seat, had to be put in the attic, as it were. After her children had grown up and were on their own so that her domestic responsibilities had become less, the woman recalled her dormant interests (she feared they were completely dead), in part through creative demands of her work. And now they were beginning to stir. Her remembering the story of Belle Rose during the time she was involved in the fairy-tale drama group was thus not an accident, but rather a very clear sign that her girlish-female traits and possibilities as well were being "resurrected."

Of course, the above does not exhaust or do complete justice to the material found in the story of Belle Rose. Depending on their individual personality and life situation, other group participants viewed other aspects as important: An only child was especially moved by Peter's loneliness; a female participant was reminded of her own old doll with its porcelain face with whom she had always had to be very careful; the father's building of a wagon for the doll reminded one male participant of the positive sides of his own father, something he had not been able to realize for a long time. The role of the dog and the animus-anima aspect of Peter and Belle Rose were also discussed at length by the group. The participants both discovered and felt deeply how differently a story can be viewed and interpreted by different people. Here, it is important that individual interpretations not be generalized or attributed to the author.

Belle Rose is an example of how a story can be rooted in the original family, the life history, the present situation, and the intrapsychic circumstances. The following story, on the other hand, written by a 25-year-old female seminar participant, was experienced by the storyteller mainly here and now, on the inner stage—on the subject level. This become even more clear through her use of the present tense.

The Elf Queen or The Power of a Strong Will

Surrounded by seven other elves, a beautiful elf queen is sitting in a blossoming field playing the flute. A prince hears her playing and follows the sound. He comes to a clearing where he spies the elves. As he steps closer to them, they suddenly disappear. He searches for them everywhere, for the beautiful elf in the middle has charmed him. But he does not find them, and decides to return the next day.

The next day as well the elves disappear when he comes closer. While he's still standing there, thinking about the beautiful elf queen, an old woman comes along and says to him: "My son, I know what puzzles you. The beautiful elf queen you have seen and cannot forget is in fact an enchanted princess. You can free her if you overcome three hindrances: First, you must cross a wild river, then defeat a dangerous dragon, and finally you must solve the hardest task of all—having the princess look you directly in the eyes. You can make it, if you really want to. But you must never give up!"

The role distribution, the acting-out, and parts of the subsequent discussion of this story may be found in more detail in the section on performing fairy tales (p. 83). There, it becomes clear that the figure of the elf queen is to be seen on the interpersonal level—on the object level.

An example of a utilitarian fairy tale is a story entitled *The Odd Couple* (see page 85), which, according to the author, serves to illustrate an inner testing of strength. It was written by a course participant overnight and acted out for the others the next day. The two hand puppets used had been made by the author himself: the well-dressed proper lady, a former lady-in-waiting at the French court (Ms. Superego), and the bum-like, primeval-looking "Neanderthal" (Mr. Id).

Part II:
Methods of
Employing Fairy Tales
in Psychotherapy

Existing or self-authored fairy tales may be used therapeutically in many different ways. Here, particularly less well-known forms of the use of fairy tales and other stories of supernatural content are discussed and presented in greater detail. The following sections should not be thought of as being mutually exclusive, but as *alternatives* that can often be combined. In some cases, after reading the fairy tale (silently or aloud), the client is struck by a particular part and can be motivated to modify it, perhaps with the help of a picture or by acting it out. In other cases, recitation leads to an increased interest in the written text; any inconsistencies can then be discussed, either alone or in a group, with respect to the storyteller's own situation, life history, and personality. The therapist should use the various methods available to further the therapy—which does not mean, however, that as many different methods as possible should be combined, either alternately or in sequence.

The choice of method should depend primarily on the personality of the individual storyteller, his or her situation, the therapeutic goals, and the setting. A look at the literature on the use of fairy tales in psychotherapy, however, shows that, for the most part, the theoretical background and the personality of the *therapist* have been viewed as decisive in the choice of methods and manners. I find it important that therapists be motivated continually to qualify their own impressions, opinions, and interpretations. The goal is to obtain a rich and deep understanding of the client's inner life. A symbol, an allegory, a metaphor, a sign—these may be absolutely clear to the therapist; but without being rooted in the life history of the client, any attempt at evoking an understanding thereof is of questionable value, and may, in fact, destroy the bond—the emotional bridge—between therapist and storyteller. The ensuing problems are then often interpreted as resistance on the part of the client, which only further complicates the situation.

For example, if I fear that my suggestion of a particular method the client is not acquainted with will upset rather than help the client, then I choose a less threatening one. Later a connection may be found that allows the material to be dealt with more deeply and creatively.

Reading and Reciting Fairy Tales

Reading Fairy Tales

Routinely suggesting that the client read fairy tales is not to be recommended. First, requests of this nature do not fit well with psychotherapeutic techniques that strive to impart insight, value the autonomy of the client, and presume a more or less complete abstinence on the part of the therapist. Second, the choice of a fitting juncture and opportune moment may be given too little attention.

Often the chance arises even during the first interview. For example, if the client is relating childhood memories, it may be convenient to discuss any story-tellers present among the client's parents, grandparents, older brothers and sisters, etc. Memories and images are sometimes then recalled which help the therapist to gain a deeper understanding of the client's childhood and subsequent development. This happens more often than therapists unacquainted with these methods would assume. In such moments the chances are higher that the suggestion of re-telling or re-reading the tales, stories, sagas, or songs of importance in childhood will be positively embraced. With so-called personal or family fairy tales (see pp. 9 and 83), I try to leave it up to the clients to determine the further route; they can recall, retell, or write them down as desired (see *Belle Rose* and *The Elf Queen* above).

If, during the course of psychotherapy, fairy-tale-like experiences are related amidst unexpected, strongly felt events, the therapist may react as follow: "That sounds like something out of a fairy tale."The positive nature of this remark is of utmost importance: So many people have been warned during their upbringing not to tell "stories." However, even a shade of insecurity or irony in the therapist's comment can make encouragement sound like the opposite.

The suggestion that fairy tales be read may be formulated and employed in various ways:

- "Do you think you might find things of interest to you in other fairy tales as well?" (general and non-directive)

- "Perhaps some further aspects would emerge if you were to re-read the fairy tales that were so important to you in your childhood." (directed at fairy tales known to and of importance to the client)

- "That's just like in the fairy tale . . ." (direct reference to a particular fairy tale not mentioned by the client)

An example:

A 28-year-old female patient began psychotherapy because of a depression she had had for two years which she—much to her own dismay—could not "shake." She was the more lively child in the family, her one year older sister being the "quiet one." The father had served for a long period as a soldier in World War II and returned from POW internment when the two girls were 8 and 9 years old. The patient described her childhood as a very happy one: She and her sister were inseparable. They grew up in the country, where despite the on-going war their very loving mother presented them with a (too?) intact world. The only important male person was one of the mother's uncles who came periodically for weekend visits. At first the girls were afraid of the uncle because of his grouchy nature and somewhat crude humor. But soon they discovered his affectionate side; they learned to play with him and tease him. If he didn't come for a while, they would inquire about him and await his next visit impatiently.

At this juncture the therapist gave the above-mentioned reference: "That's just like in the fairy tale *Snow-White and Rose-Red.*"

"How's that?" the patient responded.

"Well, the two girls in the story had similar experiences with the bear's visits . . . perhaps you could read that fairy tale, if you like."

At the next session, the patient began: "That was so strange! Although I was the one who played and romped with my uncle more, and although he took care of me more, later he actually became closer to my sister. I was so surprised in reading the fairy tale that the bear-prince marries Snow-White and that Rose-Red gets only a brother who happens to appear on the scene." (Begins to cry softly.)

After a few minutes, the therapist noted: "That deeply affects you and appears to be of great relevance to you."

The patient looked up with wide eyes; one could see that the whole matter was churning inside her: "Two years ago my sister married a childhood friend of ours . . . I was happy for her . . . for both of them . . . I loved him very much myself and wondered why he chose her, although as children the two of us had played together more than he and my sister."

With this, one factor in the causal structure for her depression became evident to her. During further therapy both the sadness over the loss and over having been slighted as well as the insufficient preparation she had received during childhood for competitive situations were worked through.

It should be emphasized that in the above-mentioned example only one parallel to the patient's situation was drawn from the fairy tale. Neither the unsolved mother-child relationship nor the confrontation with the "evil" dwarf present in the tale played a role. Also, only the object level was considered, although the patient corresponded to Rose-Red, her sister to Snow-White, the uncle and the childhood friend to the bear. On the subject level, it would have been interesting to discover whether the depressive elements were represented by the quiet sister and the absence of rivalry by the mother (on the object and subject levels, see also pages 9, 12, 23).

If a patient or a seminar participant mentions having recently read or re-read a fairy tale, I usually suggest this be repeated in my presence. If necessary, one can motivate the person by using the example of a seemingly clear sentence that receives a completely different meaning when different details are emphasized. Observe the voice tone, body position, and any gestures: These often reveal the scenes or events that particularly impress the client as well as those figures and characteristics the client identifies with and those that are rejected. The goal is to empathize, to understand how the client experiences the fairy tale, and what reactions it causes. Only then should we consider what *else* the fairy tale may have to offer.

Just reading fairy tales and sagas can often have a positive effect on the therapeutic atmosphere. Themes such as the necessity to start out on a journey, to accept a risk, to overcome dangers, to carry burdens, and in particular to forsake one thing so that another may develop—in short, the theme of *dying and becoming* (see pp. 82, 105, 120)—may influence the client. In addition, in many tales *breaking* rules or conventions leads to surprising developments. In all forms of psychotherapy that serve to evoke insight and increase functional capabilities, thoughts, fantasies, and later on trial step-wise action leading beyond previous boundaries are essential; for only in this manner can the client acquire and implement new ways of approaching life.

One client may also read aloud the original text to other participants, before the tale is acted out or imagined. Tone of voice, accentuation, and nonverbal behavior are important here. Also observe how the particular person came to assume this task, e.g., because of especially good qualities as speaker or storyteller.

This was the case of a 50-year-old female patient in a therapeutic community. The choice was clear and rational: She could read slowly, but articulately; her rich voice modulation in passages of direct quotation and her dramatic emphasis in emotionally charged scenes were appreciated by all, including the therapist. This patient was often chosen to be the *good fairy* in fairy-tale performances, and in psychodramas the understanding grandmother, the loving aunt, etc. She had never played a leading role—she had never initiated a psychodrama. Through her behavior she had assumed a position in the group and had effectively "arranged" a situation similar to that in her own life as a single woman. Both the members of her family and her colleagues at work liked her—and used her—even though she was very conscious of her own goal: She wanted to become more independent and hoped thus to gain more respect from others. The therapists then proceeded to work with her on emphasizing the ability to say no and establishing limits.

In another group a rather mediocre reader, who was also unpopular among the other members, was always given the role of storyteller. After four sessions during which he did not receive a single role, it became clear that—group dynamically speaking—he had been put on a sidetrack: He was allowed to read but not participate.

Reading of Individual Scenes or Entire Tales by the Therapist or Course Leader

This method can obviously be used only in conjunction with the proper therapy form.

In psychotherapeutic wards and therapeutic communities one can emphasize certain scenes and play down others. Direct messages may be sent to the individual patients through eye contact or gestures. This method can be very effective if the patient's background is well known and if the method is used properly—but only if perceived by the patient as concern and not as offense. Psychoanalytically speaking, this form of intervention carries with it the well-known problems of transference and countertransference.

It can be very impressive if the speaker reads the chosen fairy tale slowly and with feeling, for example, before the tale is interpreted. The following describes the method used by Verena Kast; its effectiveness is attested to by the many participants of her seminars in Europe. First, all persons attending are encouraged to make themselves comfortable. There follows a short relaxation period in which Ms. Kast suggests that everyone close their eyes during the recitation and allow the images to arise of themselves. It is important to observe the feelings and emotions that are felt at this point. Regarding the subsequent interpretation, Ms. Kast [28, 29] writes: "Of course, it would be ideal to obtain interpretations from all possible vantage points and from different people as well, if possible: Every interpretation demonstrates the personality behind it. Further, fairy tales consist of images, and images are never clear-cut; the more different levels these images contain—the more fairy-tale-like they are—the harder it is to see a clear meaning. . . . It is always possible to interpret a fairy tale in another manner. My criterion for a successful and acceptable interpretation is that it have a meaning in and of itself, i.e., in the light of the chosen vantage point all individual characteristics result in a coherent whole—or at least that the interpretation is stimulating or provocative. There is no such thing as a correct interpretation. And the interpretation of fairy tales is certainly not the only or even the most important way of dealing with them. Fantasizing and meditating upon fairy tales as well as modifying fairy-tale images seem to me to be just as important methods."

Fairy-tale imagery and the painting and drawing of such images are discussed below on pages 50ff. A great deal could be said about the question of one-sided interpretations from a personal vantage point. One should always keep this danger in mind, which is present even when the therapist attempts to offer clients both versatility and respect for their inner life. For example, in the excellent interpretations of fairy tales by Busch [3] and in Drewermann and Neuhaus's elegant series containing psychological interpretations of Grimm's Fairy Tales [8], some (very interesting) interpretations are presented simply too absolutely. The danger is that the reader might consider the particular interpretation to be the *only* true one, even though the authors fully describe their presuppositions. Even worse is when therapists force their own (or inherited) opinions and feelings upon the client: Decisive associations are missed or at least not regarded in the proper light.

Narration of Fairy Tales

Narration by the Therapist

In therapy it will often happen that clients tell a fairy tale or other stories with supernatural content. Once in a while, however, it can be better if the therapist recounts a scene from a fairy tale, perhaps even the entire tale.

Three indications should be emphasized:

- If the patient has the feeling that the particular situation is something "brand new" and "heretofore unknown," it may be advantageous to draw a parallel from a fairy tale. This spares the patient from hearing a series of examples from the life of—in the patient's eyes— "normal" people (see also page 114), which would only trivialize the problem. By noting that "even long ago people had to come to grips with such hard (painful, etc.) matters," the therapist points out that basic human conflicts and problems are often dealt with in *fairy tales*. Much as with proverbs, only repeated use causes a particular story to become a fairy tale and thus part of the cultural tradition. That some proverbs contradict each other does not prove inconsistency, but is rather an important signal that different rules can in fact be valid simultaneously. From this it follows that any attempt at solving or overcoming problems must "fit" the individual case.

- Often the therapist, by mentioning a fairy tale, can let patients know and feel that they are indeed deeply understood. Especially in therapy forms that emphasize the autonomy of the patient and the reserved position of the therapist can this underline the common emotional wavelength—without giving distracting or unnecessary insight into the personality of the *therapist*. Of course, this presumes that the therapist has properly judged the status of the therapy, the patient's life situation and personality structure. I would, however, warn against routine use: A preference for fairy tales, sagas, myths, and other stories with supernatural content may brand the therapist as a "storyteller"—actually hindering instead of furthering the therapy. With patients who consider themselves to be reality oriented (and who wish to remain so), this can easily lead to difficulties of transference and countertransference, and patient and therapist tend to lose respect for each other.

- A simple comment on the part of the therapist on a fairy tale has a stimulating effect for no other reason than than an attempt is made to overcome a seemingly hopeless situation (pp. 2, 116). In addition, telling a certain part of a tale can be stimulating in that it shows clients ways in which they—much like the heroes—can encounter and deal with problems. Thus, alternatives can also be considered, especially if clients themselves have already begun to wonder what the proper method is for their own particular personalities and what is fitting to reality.

An example:

For a 34-year-old teacher, who himself demanded of his students stamina, courage, and correctness, it was a great help to study the heroic feats of *The Valiant Little Tailor* (deceit, cunning, cleverness) and the *Musicians of Bremen* (acceptance of help, scaring someone). For only then was he able to see his own (ideologized) fixation of certain assumed traits, and that they at times indeed hindered him from tackling his real-life situation. Apparently, he did not judge fairy-tale figures as harshly or disparagingly as he did his fellow human beings.

Narration by the Client, Patient, or Course Participant

Concerning the source and form of the story, see the first section of this book (pp. 5ff.). It is of some importance here whether the client tells a well-known traditional fairy tale, a saga, a (at least partially) supernatural children's tale, a literary fable, or a personal tale. Simple conclusions, however, should be avoided. If clients recount self-authored tales, this does not automatically mean they are particularly independent, original, or eccentric because they do not repeat common knowledge. Similarly, clients telling tales from a foreign culture do not necessarily feel "foreign" in their own countries or travel unconventional paths. Interpretation of the *meaning of the narration for the narrator* can thus be successful only by taking the complete personality and the life history of the respective client—including the present situation—into account. How did the narrator come upon the tale? Did he hear it? From whom? Was that a very normal event or was it out of the ordinary? Did he read it? When, at which age, and why? What was the life situation at the time of writing the story?—these questions and others should be investigated by the therapist, albeit without necessarily directing them to the client immediately. Repeatedly querying a client directly may be interpreted as pressure or even as interrogation. Usually such matters emerge of themselves in the course of a good, warm conversation, at times of course in a rather unorderly fashion. An empathetic word—"The close relationship between the two (in *Little Brother and Sister*) seems to affect you strongly" leads more quickly to a real conversation than the question: "What is your relationship to your brother (sister)?" "That sounds like you've heard it quite often" is less prying than the direct question: "Did your grandmother tell you that story often?"

Finally, one should consider the motivation of the client for introducing the fairy tale, fable, or story into therapy. If it happens spontaneously (and this is often true with therapists who welcome fairy tales), it is also of importance to discover why the client told the tale at that particular occasion, which allows the therapist to take the present life and therapeutic situation into consideration. Also, what was said earlier about the therapist motivating clients and recommending their reading of fairy tales (p. 16) is true here for narration as well.

There are many different ways to make therapeutic use of fairy tales, selected scenes, and/or particularly important characters:

- *Comparing the recounted fairy tale or scene with the original.* Deviations, omissions, and additions can give insight into the personality-specific influence of the client or of the person who read or told the client the tale. Clients themselves are often surprised at the changes, and spontaneous comments on relatives for whom the change is or was typical often follow. Sometimes the clients suggests that there may be several varying versions of a single tale. Less often do clients immediately associate the changes with their own personality traits. But I have repeatedly had the experience that, hand in hand with a positive development of the therapy, clients do become interested and begin seeking out parallels between the changes and their own behavior.

- *Telling favorite fairy tales from childhood.* Dieckmann [6, 7] has worked with this method for several years now and has clearly shown its advantages and possibilities in his publications. Here, the links with the personality structure, the individual way of working through experiences, the life history, and the current situation of the client become clearer, whereby both earlier and present conditions can be taken into account. The timelessness of intense experiences is well known. The tendency of a person to act and react similarly over and again in life has been termed "repetition compulsion" by Freud (16), although this is, strictly speaking, not compulsive behavior.

I usually ask about the "favorite fairy tale" after discussions of early childhood memories or while discussing the family atmosphere in the early years. Often, however, this erroneously leads the client to think that it must contain something good, friendly, or pleasant; but "favorite" should be kept neutral, covering both pleasant and unpleasant stories. In any case, it is important that an element of *fascination* be present. And in general I dispense with all scientific terminology and proceed to the fairy tale with the words, "Perhaps there was a fairy tale that was very important to you in your childhood . . ." A quick answer to the effect that "We didn't tell fairy tales at my home" need not put an end to the course of the conservation: "Well, maybe there were other things—songs, stories, anecdotes, whatever" can keep the channels open. Often a fairy tale, saga, or something similar does then in fact occur in the course of further therapy, whereby the client may think it suffices to simply mention the title. In such situations it has proved useful not to demand that the entire contents be recited. Rather, by noting that "a part or a character in the story—good or bad—may have impressed you as a child," it is possible to help the clients find their own starting-points. As important as it is for work with fairy tales that one read [2] or recite [28, 29] the *entire* tale, it is even more important to therapy that unnecessary defensive attitudes be avoided. Transference and countertransference phenomena can play a large and often negative role in therapy, should dogmatic tendencies win the upper hand. Even if clients tell a fairy tale spontaneously, it is suggested that only such parts be picked out that particularly moved them, as shown through voice tone, use of direct speech, gestures, and emotional reactions (blushing, sweating, crying, etc.). It is difficult to know whether the entire development in the fairy tale or only a certain part or aspect thereof is similar to the client's own life and development, and thus "affects" him or her. And we should not forget that what is unknown and foreign is more fascinating to us and can move us more than what we know and are familiar with.

Finally, when working with favorite fairy tales of childhood, it is recommended that one always search for links between the entire story (as well as its details) and its narrator on both the object and subject level. If a clear parallel appears on the object level, e.g., concerning the family situation now or in the past, the subject level may also be productive. Much as with dreams [7, 12, 13, 27, 31, 48], here, too, we find proof for the multi-factorial determination of content. Dieckmann has given many compelling examples of this. To someone touched early on by such things, even very simple stories with only little or unclear "supernatural" content may be equally as important as the prettiest, most deeply moving fairy tale.

An example:

A rather timid 35-year-old bachelor had entered therapy for, among other things, problems of contact with others and withdrawal tendencies. He had been an only child. The father had worked away from home a great deal, and the mother had had a very fulfilling job of her own. Many of his early childhood memories are of his being alone. When questioned as to his favorite fairy tale, he replied: "No one ever told me fairy tales." But when it was pointed out that he may recall a folksong or a children's song as well, he suddenly remembered that there was, indeed, a particular song that had affected him. After a few words of encouragement, he began singing a popular German children's song:

Manikin in the forest, stands quiet and mute,

a coat of purple on his back, isn't he cute.

Tell me who can this manikin be

who stands alone among the trees,

who stands alone among the trees

in his purple coat?

He could not recall when or where he had first heard the song or who first may have sung it to him. "Maybe it was on the radio," he said. However, he then remembered that he had had a speech impediment when he was 4 or 5 years old, and that he had only spoken out loud in the presence of his mother. With others in the room he had only whispered—and then only to his mother; to strangers he wouldn't say a word. It was suggested that he search for associations, whereupon he had a number of ideas: "My mother was always very particular about my being dressed well. (laughs) Maybe that has something to do with the purple coat. I often go for long walks in the forest—it's very comforting to me there." He laughed sheepishly, then continued, obviously touched: "Even today I don't know who I really am."

At this point the patient's comments were taken up, and only later did the therapist touch on the song again, asking whether the patient was aware of the fact that the song has two more stanzas, and that actually they form a riddle concerning the rose-hip bush, as becomes apparent in the second stanza. This was new to the patient— and he was somewhat disappointed. The therapist added: "But it is our sole objective to find out who *this* man is (points to the patient) and how *he* would like to develop."

This last comment is very important, I think, as it shows that the therapist was indeed aware of the general meaning, but first wanted to discover what is important to the patient. It is, of course, questionable whether the reference to the rose-hips bush was necessary or useful at all; there may have been some profit in that it became clear what did *not* concern the patient. To associate the manikin directly with the timid bachelor would, on the one hand, fit the material as well as the patient's symptoms, but on the other hand it would reflect primarily the viewpoint of the therapist. One should be very careful about revealing to the patient such interpretations.

Continuing Fairy-Tale Beginnings

With Children and Adolescents

It was in Swedish child and adolescent psychiatry that I became acquainted with the method of continuing fairy-tale beginnings, which is used quite regularly in some places, especially in correspondence to the make-up of the original family. Depending on the age and the interests of the child or youth, one can use different materials, from "real" fairy-tale beginnings through sagas to comics (Asterix, Barbarella, etc.). The most important thing is that the client be animated to continue the tale. The indirect and thus often very revealing information one receives about the clients themselves as well as the important persons in their lives has the advantage of not injuring feelings of solidarity or loyalty. Guerin (20) has pointed out the importance of protecting feelings of loyalty in family therapy, for example, when using techniques of psychodrama. But by continuing given beginnings patients may be better able to express their feelings, and often very creative attempts at overcoming problems evolve; these can, if the therapist reacts skillfully enough, lead to a deeper relationship between therapist and client, to greater trust, and to a better therapy result.

A nine-year-old boy, who was for modern times a little too much of a "good boy," was referred by his school for testing and perhaps therapy because of difficulties in learning and concentration. His very concerned and cooperative parents came with him to the psychiatric outpatient clinic. It soon became apparent that he was being taunted by his peers and was very scared, but that he had never dared to tell his parents or his teachers about this. The youngest of three children, he was somewhat babied and overprotected at home—for which he was secretly punished by his two older brothers. During the course of several conversations and in the games with the sand-box material of the *Erica Foundation* [21] he always remained the well-behaved, well-adjusted good little boy. The psychologist then tried to reach him with a fairy-tale beginning: "Once upon a time, long ago, there lived a king, a queen, and their three children. Now, the youngest prince . . ." Thereupon, the boy wrote simple stories corresponding to his age: ". . . watched his brothers play soccer. He was not allowed to play with them, since he was too small and too weak. Once, when the king and queen were away, there came a thunderstorm, and lightning struck the oldest two princes . . . and when the king came home, he swore at the heavens and he too was struck by lightning. Then the queen came and saw all that had happened, and she screamed and was so sad that she fell over dead . . . *and that was the end of the story.*" Two other beginnings were completed in a similar manner and ended equally with the death of all persons involved—only the youngest prince, who was always a spectator, surviving. And the same sentence always came at the end: ". . . and that was the end of the story."

Characteristically, only external and quite often higher powers were the destructive factors. The final survivor always died of shock or grief. The family members did not harm one another.

For the therapist it was surprising that these aggressive impulses, otherwise not always easy to tap, became evident so quickly through the simple offer of a surreal/unreal fairy-tale world not bound to realistic description. Thereafter, activities of the boy with both younger children and later with peers were built into the therapy in small steps.

With Adults

My work with adults has shown that suggestions to continue a story are welcomed if they are made at the proper time and in the proper manner. Here are two examples.

Example 1

A 40-year-old male began therapy during an existential crisis because of problems with his self-esteem. "I don't have a goal anymore. I have the feeling that I'm no longer of any use. At home and at work everything would get along fine without me. I don't really do much anymore. I used to be a good, reasonable, hard-working person." The patient and his older brother had assumed control of the firm founded by the father after the latter's death three years previously. As children and as colleagues they had always gotten along quite well. The father had loved both sons very much and had praised each for his individual abilities and achievements. For about a year after the father's death they had continued to manage the company together as their father would have. Then something happened. The patient reported on this as always in a composed, very matter-of-fact manner: "For the past year and a half things haven't worked out between my brother and myself as well as in the past. I couldn't do anything right in his opinion. He always criticized any suggestions I made. But if I, on the other hand, made even the slightest comment on or wanted to supplement a plan of his, he was hurt and got very angry. Finally, I decided to leave the company and took my present job in management. Things there were all right until this feeling of uselessness and the concentration problems came upon me.

(Pause) It's so strange because we always got along so well. That's what made our father so optimistic about the future. In our discussions I was always concerned with the company and nothing else, with our daily cooperation on company matters . . . (he now sounded somewhat annoyed) . . . I've tried everything . . . (now angry) Damn, it's as though it's jinxed!"

The patient paused. While pondering the fact that there were no feelings of sadness amongst those of anger, the therapist came upon an image of the two brothers separated by a large, unbridgeable gap—a gap once filled by the affection of the father toward both. Now, through the competitive situation, the gap had grown ever larger. Instead of directly mentioning the sadness, which may not have been experienced directly, the therapist said (and the session was drawing to a close) in a slow, quiet voice:

Once there were two princes,

and they loved each other so much,

they could not come together,

for the water was much too deep.

Now, the younger prince . . .

(in a normal tone of voice) Perhaps you could find a few quiet minutes to continue the story and bring your version along to the next session."

At the next session, the patient started off by taking up the story. Apparently the shift from lovers (in the original story) to brothers had not caused any problems. During the course of repeated unsuccessful attempts to continue the story, he felt first angry and then sad. The feelings of sorrow were not only accepted by the therapist, but furthered in the light of the earlier (pleasant) feelings of solidarity with the brother and loss at the father's death. Thus, it became possible to pose the question whether the brothers had ever actually spoken of how sad it was that the they no longer had their father who had loved them each in a particular way, and how it was possible that they had entered into a competition with each other which earlier had not been necessary.

By taking a stance of showing understanding for all concerned, the therapist had a role similar to the father. But because a long-term therapy was not planned, this aspect could not be addressed further. Though he did not return to the position in the family firm, the patient did eventually speak with his brother about the aspect of sorrow in a good and deep conversation that promoted new feelings of solidarity. Although, or perhaps because, a complete restoration of the earlier relationship did not take place, the patient's ability to work and be creative returned, and his feelings of uselessness gradually disappeared.

This was an example of a situation on the object level, i.e., the *actual* relationship of the two brothers to each other and to their father. The next example concerns the subject level.

Example 2

The 38-year-old female patient had lost her job as a secretary two years prior to beginning therapy. Several years previously she had worked abroad as a foreign correspondence secretary. When the company she was working for went bankrupt, she was still single and went to live with her aged mother some 120 km away, who subsequently "took her for herself." The woman experienced this safe but dependent life as very unsatisfying, yet she was unable to escape the true helplessness of her mother. In the course of time she suffered an increasing loss of concentration and became disquieted, though she continued to be friendly to her mother. Both her older brother as well as her sister and brother-in-law did not take her seriously. The clever brother-in-law acted as though she did not exist, once forgetting to pick her up as arranged for a picnic and not even bothering to apologize. The patient was not able to defend herself and make her needs known. One day she became confused and—according to the relatives and a doctor prsent—spoke with herself and with some invisible being in the left corner of the room.

The patient was hospitalized twice in the following year and a half and received neuroleptics. Following the second stay, she was referred to a preparatory course for a more intensive therapy. She felt "relaxed on the outside, but on the inside uneasy, unsteady, paralyzed." A 20-hour therapy series was agreed upon. There she reported all objective things completely realistically, but was simply unable to open up on her subjective experiences. In the eighth session the therapist mentioned this, which resulted in a considerable disquietude in the patient; she turned herself repeatedly to the left, nodded her head sometimes, bulged her eyes, and could no longer concentrate on the conversation.

Therapist (accepting what was apparently present for the patient): There's something over there I can't see.

Patient looks repeatedly back and forth from the left corner to the therapist, and then says softly): Yes. . .yes. . .

Therapist: I would like to see it too.

Patient: No . . . no. (looks quickly to the left) I can'tlet that happen . . . They stop me.

Therapist: Are there more than one? . . . I would like to meet them.

Patient (looks at therapist amazed): Really? (now quickly and softly) I've got to get rid of them . . .

Therapist: That would surely make them sad or perhaps angry.

Patient: Yes, they'd become very big and would threaten me.

Therapist: It's too bad I can't see them . . .

Patient: He's like a small dragon, similar anyway, and she like a small snake . . . and when they become angry and big, he spews fire and she venom and she looks at me very devilishly . . . no, I can't take it any longer!

Therapist: I would like to see what happens between you three . . . (short pause). . . perhaps I could get a better picture of it all if you would make a story out of it. (The patient looks at the therapist with astonishment—though not negatively.) I'll write down the beginning for you: "Once upon a time, when the animals and humans still understood each other, there was a small dragon, a small snake, and a woman. When the dragon was angry, it became very big and spewed fire; the snake became sinister and spewed venom. One day the woman . . ."—so there's the beginning. (He gives the patient the sheet of paper.) Would you like to go on with the story?

The continuation of the story was very short. The patient read it aloud at the therapist's request.

Patient: One day the woman couldn't stand it any longer and went to find someone to get rid of or transform the snake and the dragon. Thereupon, the two became even bigger and angrier, and the woman was afraid and completely distressed and wanted only to run away. But everywhere she went the dragon and the snake followed. She couldn't work or do anything. She was completely desperate; she didn't know how she could live on like that.

Therapist: If the woman were to commit suicide in her desperation, do you think the dragon and the snake would then go to someone else? Or do they belong to her personally?

Patient: I think they're only there for her.

Therapist: Do you think they know that they too will disappear if they drive the woman to despair? It's too bad the three of them can't get along with each other. (gestures to the left side) I could sure use a fire-spewing dragon and a poisonous and cunning snake myself (note: cunning and not sinister), for example, tomorrow in my meeting with the administration and the representatives of the psychotherapy department.

The patient looks at the therapist with amazement and shakes her head.

Therapist (now directing attention away from the story and to the patient): Yeah, too bad they can't get along . . .

At the beginning of the next session the patient declared that "both of them" had reminded her (to her own amazement) not to forget the upcoming session. "It's strange because they used to forbid me to even mention it"—something the patient had indeed not done during inpatient care.

Therapist: They speak to you?

Patient: Not so that I can hear them, but I know what they think and what they want from me.

As the therapy continued, the dragon and the snake were always considered as immanently present beings. Sometimes I noted that these dragon and snake qualities were missing in her behavior. Then these themes disappeared for several months, and only practical matters such as her finishing a course, beginning work at a research institute, visits with the mother, etc., were in the forefront. About six months later the patient said, with a slightly embarrassed grin but with bright eyes: "A couple of days ago I was a snake and a little bit of a dragon, too."

Therapist (with intense interest and approval): Uh-huh.

Patient: A neighbor came over and entered my apartment without knocking . . . he does that sometimes. He was a patient with me at the hospital. I used not to say anything, but this time I told him that I had to get ready for work, which wasn't exactly true. I thought that was bad of me. But when he didn't go right away, I hissed at him whether he hadn't understood that I didn't have the time right then. He looked at me strangely, too, when I said: "By the way, you could knock before you come in." I was, of course, somewhat unsure whether I had been too harsh, but generally I was pleased with myself.

In this case the dragon and the snake were approached in therapy on the subject level—as projected inner elements of the patient: as possibilities the patient lacked. Of course, the connection to the mother and sister still had to be worked through; but the revelation of the patient's ability to be a dragon and a snake seemed to her to be more important.

Changing and Modifying Existing Texts

On the basis of the above-mentioned example, we can now discuss the modification of a self-authored story. The same patient thus received a sheet of paper with her own continuation of the fairy-tale beginning given above.

Therapist: How would you continue the story? You may choose yourself the place in the story at which a different development begins.

A week later the patient read the following:

Once upon a time, when the animals and humans still understood each other, there was a small dragon, a small snake, and a woman. When the dragon was angry, it became very big and spewed fire; and the snake became sinister and spewed venom. One day the woman couldn't stand it any longer and went to find someone to get rid of or transform the snake and the dragon. Thereupon, the two became even bigger and angrier, and the woman was afraid and completely distressed and wanted only to run away. (Note the changes now in the story with respect to the above version.) But she knew that would not be possible. In her despair she screamed at them: "If you keep on tormenting me, then I can't live on . . . and if I die, so do you." The snake and the dragon looked at each other in complete surprise. The woman continued: "I'm so afraid of you and I don't know myself what's the matter with you when you become so angry and sinister. The fact is I could use your help and strength against my relatives and otherwise." Thereupon, the dragon said: "You want our help and at the same time you want to get rid of us or have us transformed?" The snake added: "Apparently you think you're smarter than I am—but you can't fool me!" The woman said: "Don't you understand? That's what I sometimes need, your smartness—and the strength of the dragon. Please, tell me what you want from me in exchange?" The snake and the dragon looked at each other; they had grown a little smaller now and didn't look quite so horrible. "First of all, stop trying to get rid of us," the snake said, and the dragon added with a hiss: "And when you want my help, you'll have to ask for it." The woman promised this, and slowly but surely they gained trust in one another; in difficult situations they would confer as to how they could best work together and help each other. Sometimes the woman was still afraid when the dragon became too big and spewed fire—though she was more afraid now for those he spewed his fire upon. And it still sometimes felt a bit strange to her when the snake hatched her venomous plans. But at least she was able to talk to the two and to deal with them. And when she reminded the snake or the dragon of the consequences of their actions for the three of them, they even gave in somewhat—now that they were not only being taken seriously, but had a useful role. So they lived happily ever after together in the same house.

This is an example of an individually adapted therapy for a primarily psychogenic psychosis. Thinking up and modifying her story in a successive reduction of the projections seems to have helped this woman. Of course, such methods cannot be generalized, and therefore are not to be seen as valid therapeutic forms for psychosis or schizophrenia. In my opinion, it suffices if fairy tales or personal stories are employed in special cases of psychosis in order to gain an inroad into the inner world of the patient—as it were, to take influence from within and without.

Another example:
During the second round of acting out *Rumpelstiltskin* at a training workshop, the content of the fairy tale was changed considerably (see p. —) After I had tolerated this expressly and showed it to be profitable, the following discussion made clear that other participants as well had strong desires to recast the fairy tale. Thus, I requested that all persons think up their own version for the next day. Here are two very different results:

Once upon a time there was a miller, who was very poor but had a beautiful daughter. Now it happened that he, as he came to speak with the king, to impress him said: "I have a daughter who can spin gold out of flax." The king said to the miller: "That is an art indeed that I like! If your daughter is as talented as you say, bring her tomorrow to my castle—I would like to test her." And when the maid was brought to him, he led her to a chamber full of flax, gave her a spinning wheel and reel and said: "So begin, and if you do not spin this flax into gold by morning, you shall die." (Up to here we are dealing with the original story of the Grimm Brothers.) And the miller's daughter cried out in despair: "But I can never do that!" Whereupon the king said crossly: "But your father told me so." Then the maid declared: "My father always boasts of me, but I cannot make gold out of flax." "Then return home. But I shall punish your father," the king said. "Oh, please do not do that, Your Highness. He is a poor man. I shall leave my home and shall tell him why. That shall be enough of a punishment for him." And the king was touched by her honesty and her intercession on the part of her father and let her go. She told the father that he had gone too far this time, and then left for another land. There she worked very diligently and gained many friends.

The storyteller was a single woman who lived alone, the favorite daughter of her father. Her decision to leave her parents' house had been a difficult one for her. She was surprised herself by the way she had chosen to end the story: In reality she had a number of very nice colleagues but no real friends. She thought this was due to her inability to defend herself when praised too highly; it caused her the most pain when she had to distance herself as a result. At work she had no difficulties defending her interests, but privately it was a different matter.

Another participant followed the original text up to the meeting with Rumpelstiltskin:

. . . And you can imagine how happy the queen was when she heard the name and when soon thereafter the manikin entered and asked: "So, Your Highness, what is my name?" (from here on the text differs from the original) And she said: "Manikin, I know your name! But you have spun gold from flax three times and have let me guess your name when I wept in despair. Now that I have a child myself, I can understand how you wanted to have a living being for your own. I'll make you a offer: You can stay at our court, come and go as you please. You may play with my daughter (note that the king is mentioned nowhere, and the storyteller has determined of her own accord the sex of the child—in the original fairy tale only the *child* is mentioned). And because you know so much and have so many abilities, I shall ask you often for your advice. Well, what do you think?" The dwarf answered: "You just say that because in fact you do *not* know my name. Say my name or give me the child immediately!" So the queen spoke in a low and serious voice: "I do know your name. Rumpelstiltskin." And the dwarf was amazed and did not know whether he should explode, run away or whatever. The queen said: "Remember my offer,I meant it seriously." Rumpelstiltskin looked from the queen to the child and inquired: "And I can really come and go as I please?" "Yes," the queen assured him, "and play with my daughter and help her and advise me." The queen stretched out her hand to the manikin and added: "I give you my word." Rumpelstiltskin hesitated a bit, but having no better alternative finally agreed.

This 25-year-old female participant reported spontaneously that her version of the story fulfilled a childhood wish: She had always considered it unjust that Rumpelstiltskin was torn apart and had to die, even though he had been so helpful and motivated to make compromises by the fear and the sadness of the miller's daughter and later queen. She was very pleased with the ending of her version. When asked "Why do you think the child was a little girl?" she could only answer that the child had always been a girl for her. In the following the group discussed whether this had to do with the woman's own child wish—preferably a girl—and its meaning on the subject level. Three main aspects were treated: (1) How the woman dealt with the "little girl" in herself: In addition to the mother-caretaker part, what about the development of her own resources, her creative possibilities—the little girl in her—by skill or by deceit? (2) One other female group member asked how she dealt with her desires to *possess*, to have something for her own (Rumpelstiltskin wanted to possess a living being for himself, the queen wanted to keep her child). (3) Another member said: "For me "spinning flax into gold" has something sensual, erotic, and sexual about it. People used to sleep on straw. I see in Rumpelstiltskin an expression of the sexuality of the miller's daughter, who can deal with it only after having given it a name. I like the way your story closes very much, even if I myself cannot always come to grips with these parts of myself." At this juncture the group leader said: "It was a wishful ending, perhaps even something that must be particularly watched after if it is not to be lost."

The storyteller was completely surprised by the comment of another female participant, who said with a laugh, "What do you think the king would say about the fact that your queen didn't even consult him before making Rumpelstiltskin the offer?" After a while the storyteller said, with reference to the fairy tale, that the king was apparently interested only in the gold; he is no longer mentioned after the wedding and seemed to play a subordinate role. This was confirmed by re-reading the fairy tale, which relieved the storyteller of the pressure on her. Then she said: "Nevertheless, the matter of deciding on one's own, of taking on the responsibility alone . . . and forgetting that someone else is also concerned, does sound familiar. I recognize myself there. If someone accuses me of this, I can always deny it. But if the interests of others are hurt, then I do feel bad about it."

This aspect of assuming responsibility and asserting one's own tendencies brought the discussion back to the object level. If it does not occur on its own, it is often advantageous that the group leader guide the discussion such that practical and pragmatic concerns for the external reality of the "story-reteller" be handled last. This makes it easier for the person to return from the inner trip (especially from the realms of the supernatural), and it makes the step from the "surplus reality" of the fairy-tale world [36] to the real world outside of the group or therapy situation somewhat smaller.

Changing and modifying existing fairy tales, sagas, and myths does not, of course, appeal to all, especially not to those who love and appreciate them just as they are. Popular fairy tales are often thought to be especially worthy of being retained in the given form. If a traditional story is to be used in therapy in the traditional form, then it would be absurd to suggest changing it. But if changing the tale can in fact further the course of therapy, I see no need not to proceed out of respect for the original version. One should also emphasize that the "author" changes the tale only for his or her own purposes; it is not changed for all of society nor is it in any way being "perverted." The different personal variations become especially clear in group work that is lead in a relaxed and open manner—and nowhere else does the simplicity, clearness, and symbolic meaning of the original tale emerge more clearly and elegantly. The so-called collective unconscious [27] is not rendered banal by individual variations, on the contrary, it is often amplified and enriched.

From changing and varying fairy tales to the next section is only a small step.

Inventing Fairy Tales

Here, the suggestions given above on contents as well as on motivating the client are unnecessary. Self-authored fairy tales may, however, be divided into private fairy tales from earlier times (see pp. 9, 83) and those thought up after participation in psychodrama, after work with childhood memories, with guided affective imagery, or with a fairy-tale performance. Also, fairy tales arising from daydreams are welcome. Of course, the therapist always has the possibility of mentioning, proposing, suggesting, or even actively supporting the invention and writing of fairy tales. The latter is particularly well regarded in psychotherapeutic communities as furthering to the therapy. In one ward, for example, the personnel more or less intensively suggested that fables and fairy-tale-like stories concerning the therapists and the ward itself be written for the group gatherings. The patients could best write and develop tales when no one from the personnel was present. The duty nurse indeed had trouble holding herself back when the group laughed, gave her pregnant glances, or even invited her to play along.

There are a number of matters to consider when using self-authored fairy tales in therapy. First, what are the authors saying about themselves, their present or past surroundings, their symptoms, and the therapeutic situation? Before therapists comments on or interpret anything, they should first consider whether this would truly help the patient. The time and place of comments, and particularly the amount and the way in which they are made, can determine whether or not the patient can accept the intervention and assimilate it. The following three examples are intended to illustrate how individual and group forms may arise and contribute to a deeper self-insight on the part of the patient-storyteller—and a deeper understanding of the patient on the part of the therapist.

Example 1

In an encounter group with the theme "Magical Content in Guided Affective Imagery," the drawings of one female participant contained a big and a small fish. In the subsequent discussion (not of further interest here) the different symbolic, allegorical, *and* practical aspects of fish were considered in detail. Several sayings were mentioned: "Small fish, good fish," "Fresh as a fish," etc. A pedagogic formula was even remembered: "Keep your hands on the table and sit as quiet as a fish." After seeing a reproduction of the painting "Der große Freund" (The Big Friend) by Sulamith Wülfing, which depicts a little girl protruding out of the mouth of a dragon-like fish-head, a female participant wrote the following fairy tale (the original text including the author's punctuation is reproduced here):

> Once upon a time there was a little girl; she lived in a garden that was very big, so big in fact that when standing at the old well at the middle of the garden one could not see the wall that surrounded it. The wall was covered with moss and ivy and a few flowers and there was no exit, no gate, no ladder, no window. And behind the wall reigned endless darkness. The garden was dominated by powerful figures who, it was said, were black as the night and had devastated the entire countryside beyond th garden, so that neither wind nor water nor plant nor animal existed there. The king of the garden, it was told, had disappeared on the day the dark figures had appeared. That was also the day the little girl was born and thus she had never seen the king. Every evening when it became dark and the mother had given the little girl a good-night kiss, the girl tiptoed barefoot to her window, opened it quietly, and called to her friend, the cat, who came running with sparkling eyes. The little girl understood the language of the animals and the plants. Then both of them climbed down over the roof and ran stealthily behind the big trees to the old well. The cat sprang as always to her look-out position, a big tree, and the girl leaned over the surface of the water in which the stars danced wildly and shone brightly and the water began to rush and roar. Then her dear od friend came up from the deep, a huge, very old fish stemming from the time when the fish and dragons looked very similar. The two of them had experienced a lot together, and in this night a plan concocted long ago was to be enacted. For years the fish and the girl had swum night for night down the underground river to the sea where a huge tree stood. In the crown of the tree lived a butterfly. In many a dark night the fish, the tree, and the butterfly had found out where the stone lay, the only way through which—if picked up by a human—the wall surrounding the garden could be opened and the entire country be bright again and full of life. Then the king would return to the garden. The evening was cool and the girl shivered, but more from fear than from cold, for she would have to go through the darkness alone tonight and leave her friends. She thought once again of her cat, who was watching out at the well, and of her mother, who had no idea what was happening, then she left her safe place in the large fish mouth and began to climb the tree. She set herself on the back of the butterfly and they began a long flight into the realm of darkness. The butterfly flew silently through the night and they came to a cave where the stone was supposed to be. The girl made her way in-

side through a small slit and was surrounded by such darkness as she had never before experienced. She felt her way across the floor, it seem unending to her, and then she suddenly felt something round in her hand and there was a loud bang and a light so bright that the girl had to close her eyes. When she opened them again, everything looked different. She was standing before a large gate that was opened wide and she looked into the garden. The sun shone and everything was in blossom. Colorful butterflies were flying through the air and as the girl came closer to them to ask them what had happened, she noticed that she could no longer understand the language of the animals and the plants. That made her sad, but then she noticed that the paths were full of people in bright, colorful clothes, and they laughed and danced. The girl ran further and there she saw the king. He came up to her, took her in his arms and said with a smile: "There you are, finally . . ."

Since this fairy tale could not be discussed in the group, and thus the story-teller did not have the possibility of working through the tale, I will not mention here my own thoughts and interpretations. But perhaps it can still serve for the reader as an example of how to approach such a story.

Taking a look at the contents, the details included, and also more formal matters (syntax, vocabulary, punctuation), while at the same time allowing the story to "soak in," the reader will have certain associations. Read the text through once again slowly, or have it read to you slowly, letting the images arise of themselves. "What appeals to me in this tale?" "What scenes, parts, persons, or actions are particularly touching and in what way?" Such inner participation can lead to partial insight about oneself. But only in view of the life history and the thoughts of the *author* should speculations on the meaning and associations to the *author's* life be made. If a reader has a particular idea or interpretation that, as it were, elbows it way into consciousness, then the content of that interpretation most certainly concerns the *reader* and his or her own situation and background. Whether this is as relevant to the author of the tale can only be discovered together with this person on the basis of his or her life. I chose the tale above quite intentionally in order to emphasize these aspects, and dispensed with an interpretation of the many possible meanings because of the lack of information at our disposal. Nevertheless, we can gain a lot by allowing the images and the ideas to work within us.

Example 2

During an intensive course on "Fairy Tales and Performing Fairy Tales in Psychotherapy," I mentioned that it would be nice and perhaps good for all involved if someone were to think up a fairy tale during the course. This way the group would have the opportunity to perform a story according to a text or script. Two male participants, Mr. R., about 30 years old, and Mr. U., some two or three years older, surprised the group by writing a piece within two days in their relatively little spare time. In order to better understand the elements at work here, the reader must know something of the development of the group dynamics and of the experiences of the authors during the course of the previous days; see in this respect the section "Free Improvisation of Fairy Tales" on page 102ff. Here, we are concerned only with the writing of this "epic" (as I would like to call it) entitled *Philipp and Eberhard*. For a description of the subsequent performance of the tale, see page 90ff.

Before beginning Mr. R. and Mr. U. explained that it was now no longer possible to determine who had written what part of the story. They also said that the two heroes did not correspond to the two authors, but that the story as a whole was dedicated to the group. The text was originally written by longhand, and in the later typewritten version I had at my disposal I discovered only one change in content, which I will go into in more detail below. The form, structure, etc., of the original manuscript have been retained down to the last detail.

Philipp and Eberhard

Once there were two brothers whose father was king of a powerful nation.
One day he arranged for a feast to be held.
The Queen of Aquitania had come to visit.
Her father had died and her mother too;
so she assumed the throne very young, alone, but resolute.
She wanted very much to meet men, as she was looking for a husband,
and she thought of Eberhard, the handsome son of the neighbor.
So they sat at the table, the king, his wife,
the guest from Aquitania, Philipp, and Eberhard.
Philipp, who sucked his thumb and sat daydreaming,
thought about the heroic times and heroic deeds.
He loved Odysseus, that cunning man,
but he also loved David, who slew Goliath.
Eberhard sat there grumbling, full of stubbornness,
he didn't like sitting, his thoughts began to roam.
Suddenly the chancellor entered: "Your Majesty, bad news!
Our evil neighbor, Herrmann, is threatening our border!"
"Chancellor, Sir, let us eat, the fowl tastes so good,
don't bother us at dinner, bring us better news."
The older son moaned:
So was typical of Father, he never did like to take action,
he loved eating, music and his bed,
and when he really *had* to rule, he didn't really want to.

The meal continued merrily, then the Chancellor came again:
"Your Majesty, pray listen, that impudent, evil Herrmann
has burned down our border city as if at war!"
The king said: "That's horrible, come here and eat.
Tomorrow we will confer, we'll find a solution."
Eberhard could not constrain himself, he stood up inflamed:
"Father, your inactivity, it depresses me so!
Let me do something, I beg of you, give me an army!"
The father only growled: "Boy, what's the matter with you?
War is a matter for men.
Go now, take a seat, eat in peace and enjoy the dancing!
We have a guest from afar, go and meet her."
But Eberhard was angry:
"Father, I am no longer a child!
I am the heir to the throne, I want to do something—now!"
The king did ignore him and Eberhard went red with anger:
"Then I shall go off and travel round the world!"
The mother spoke: "My son, we love you so much.
You'll break our hearts if you leave in hate."
And Eberhard said: "Madam, give me my freedom!
I must go away, I can no longer stay with you!"
The king spoke: "Well! You shall not get the throne.
But you shall receive three jewels, the entire treasure of the land."
Philipp asked: "Brother, why must you go?
I like it very much here at home."
"My little one," the answer came quickly,
"what do you know about freedom, about boundless joy."
And so he left. The parents bemoaned his absence,
but the Queen of Aquitania was lost in thought.
So the son roamed the world and never stopped,
he came through villages cities, turned toward the South.
And there he became tired, and hungry, and so very thirsty,
until he found an inn, called "The Full Mug."
The innkeeper, a squat man, invited him in.
There he drank seven days long, the wine tasted so good.
But finally he was down, down under the table, I mean,
then he woke up with a hangover, his head a buzzing.

The innkeeper spoke: "Sir, the bill, I'd like it paid now!"
Eberhard understood and paid, that is, he wanted to pay.
But he didn't have a penny and so he reached into his belt,
for there he had stored the jewels of his father.
He gave one to the innkeeper and moved on, ashamed;
for now he had wasted a third of his inheritance.
He roamed through the forest and valleys, felt quite alone,
until he came to a hut, called "The Green Wreath,"
where played women merrily to dance.
He went in, and soon he sat full merriment
and a woman, scantily clad, offered him her red mouth.
So they went to her room and fell into her bed
and Rosalind, that was her name, was truly very nice to him.
He loved her, and she offered him her body.
She laughed abundantly, but finally freed herself from his embrace,
rose, went to the door and said to him:
"You're a noble warrior on the battlefield of desire,
but other guests are waiting, do understand."
Eberhard was downhearted, lay alone in bed,
oh that Rosalind, she was not really nice, not really.
And then he had to pay—she even wanted his money!
And Eberhard understood and paid, that is, he wanted to pay,
but he didn't have a penny and so he reached into his belt
and gave that girl the second beautiful jewel.
So he moved on, ashamed, having wasted two-thirds of his inheritance.
He came to a field, there someone was wailing,
he strained to see where this wailing was coming from.
There he saw a beautiful maid in a long, white dress;
blond hair framed her face.
An evil, black knight was dragging her along,
he had robbed her and wanted his ransom.
And Eberhard understood and paid, that is, he wanted to pay,
but he didn't have a penny and so he reached into his belt.
He gave the black knight his last jewel.
Yet he was very, very happy, as the maid was so fair.
But she did say: "My boy, I thank you so much,
but I love another, do understand,

I love another," spoke she and left him standing there.
He cried bitterly, roamed the world,
lost, alone, without means, hungry and tired.
Then he came to a farmer with a thousand swine
who gave him to eat and a place to sleep.
But he had to tend the swine in the field.
And so he lived there several weeks long,
as a keeper of swine—he, the son of a king!
He thought of his parents and his small brother,
and deep was his desire to return home.
The king, in the meantime, was sick with grief,
his heir had left him, full of hate and thankless.
The evil neighbor, Herrmann, was suffering him sorely,
had marched into the king's land with a large army.
The king was despondent, the people asked: "What shall we do?"
Then came Philipp, the thumbsucking boy:
"I shall," he said, "go fight against Herrmann the Warrior.
I shall triumph, I shall save my land, my homeland."
The king wanted to hold him back, his only remaining son,
the mother wrung her hands, but Philipp went off.
He approached Herrmann: "Neighbor, why are you pressuring us?
Be peaceful, Wild One, come and let us be friends!"
But Herrmann was wrathful and evil was his eye:
"What do you want, boy, beat it, your land is my desire."
And Philipp said: "I'm sure that is your desire—
but first you shall have to fight against this young man."
And he pointed to himself. Herrmann laughed loud and strong,
which did cut Philipp to the quick.
Bravely he said: "Come, fight with me, Sir!
If you win, you shall receive our entire kingdom.
But if I win, I shall receive *your* kingdom!"
And Herrmann said: "Fine, this challenge I shall meet.
I shall make pudding of you, you brat!"
So they began fighting. O woe, that shouldn't have been!
For Herrmann was a giant and carried a huge sword,
and Philipp slight and a homebody.
But he was clever, he ran away, and

Herrmann chased him with ridicule:
"Hey, boy, stop now! I'll get you soon,
and when I get you, then shall I also have your kingdom!"
Philipp lured him into a room of mirrors
and dodged and made himself small.
And when Herrmann came, he saw before him a huge image:
A wild man with a sword and gigantic shield.
He lurched for him—but only a mirror broke,
and Herrmann fell into a deep hole.
And thus he was caught by the cunning of a boy,
and Herrmann was furious and bellowed: "Dammit!"
And Philipp laughed: "Take heart, Wild One!
I shall let you live, as I do not want to (cannot) kill."
And so he freed Herrmann from the hole,
let him keep his lands, invited him even to dine.
So there they sat at the table, the king, his wife
and the proud young hero.
And Herrmann, the tamed neighbor, appeared, in good spirits,
at his arm his daughter, of fair appearance.
She blushed upon seeing Philipp, for he pleased her well,
he was so young and happy and full of cunning.
She thanked him for saving the life of her father.
Philipp, as well in love with her, shyly spoke to her:
"My dear, beautiful maid, tell me your name.
Mine is Philipp, I hope you like it."
She said: "I am called Lisa." And he said: "A fine name."
So Philipp went to her parents and asked for her hand.
It was given him, and they all rejoiced,
Herrmann was satisfied, the king much more.
They celebrated the engagement with a feast
—but in no time did the mood change.
There came a man in rags, bent over like a farmer,
and when the rags fell from him, there stood—poor Eberhard.
Who fell onto his knees, eyes full of tears,
and said: "Father and dear Mother mine,
I return destitute, downtrodden and full of woe.
Please accept me as loser and let me join you again.

The parents rejoiced, the heir had returned,
and they wanted to hear all that he had done and experienced.
And so he told of the inn, of the beautiful whore,
of the thieving knight and of his pain of love.
Too he told of working, deeply ashamed he revealed
that he had tended swine! They shook in astonishment, what!
The king was full of consternation, took his son by the arm,
drew him to his breast, his voice now warm.
"My dear Eberhard,
I too was not a very wise man,
I let things go instead of going at things.
Now you are again my heir, sit down at my side!
Let us rejoice thrice over, today is a true feast!"
But Philipp despaired, his elder brother again the heir!
Lisa took him tenderly in her arm and spoke to him:
"What do you need an inheritance for, you've got me,
and I am the heir to the kingdom you have earned!"
So Philipp was content, went to Eberhard,
hugged him kindly, and there was much rejoicing.
And thus things ended well, for that is the end,
and in a year's time Herrmann was a grandpa . . .
And Eberhard again set out on a journey
and traveled to Aquitania . . .

After Mr. R. and Mr. U had alternately read the entire story, there were a few minutes of silence in the group. Then a broad discussion seemed to be in the offing, which I stopped, fearing that a free unfolding necessary to an acting-out of the tale could suffer from working through the material verbally beforehand. Nevertheless, the participants felt a great need to express their feelings, and since the last session for that day was drawing to a close, I suggested that everyone who wanted to was welcome to make a comment on a detail in the story or to make a suggestion. Mr. R. and Mr. U. were of the opinion that they themselves had done enough, and if the story were performed, they did not want to play Eberhard and Philipp.

One member did not like Eberhard's telling everything after his return home; he himself would have refused to do any such thing. A female member of the group wanted to continue the story to see whether Eberhard and the Queen of Aquitania would get together—three other persons in the group, however, were against such an action, as they had the feeling that the story as it stood was more dramatic. I myself stumbled over the phrase "*cannot* kill," as it originally stood, since I would have expected "do not *want* to kill." Perhaps this is an example of the importance of the group leader's position, as this was the only place in the story that was subsequently changed by the authors in the typewritten version. The smaller the ego strength of the participants, the more carefully the therapist has to be with his or her own opinions and impressions.

Finally, each participant had the opportunity to sketch shortly a scene, character, or part of the plot of particular importance to him or her. In order to maintain the tension for the acting-out on the next day, I closed the session by appealing to the group not to discuss the story in the meantime. The motivation of the members as well as their ego strength were apparently very high: They indeed did refrain from further discussions.

A short note on the literary quality: Critique did not arise during the first reading, since all—the participants, the group leader, and co-leader—were too captivated by the story to pay much attention to grammatical or stylistic problems. Indeed, when a story is being used in therapy or for imparting insight into personal matters or group dynamics, its literary quality is of secondary importance. On the other hand, it is understandable that the defects of such an attempt do bother some people. While working on this manuscript I had to hold myself back repeatedly from trying to "improve" this epic by changing the verse or the punctuation. But the unchanged original version is more important than any literary scruples. However, I can now understand that the Grimm Brothers were not always able to resist changing and "improving" upon some of the tales they gathered.

Example 3

A further type of fairy-tale invention is possible in the group as a whole. Here, too, I would not suggest initiating such an activity routinely: Though it may improve the group dynamics and the relationships among the members, it hardly furthers group cohesion and a trustful cooperation. If the beginnings of fairy-tale invention arise spontaneously in the group and the majority of the members express interest, this direction can be pursued. Group invention is also possible after having deviated considerably from the original text of a fairy tale or after having acted out a tale, or when the majority of the group is not happy with a part or the end of a particular fairy tale. But one should strive to avoid both unnecessary injuries to individual members and extremely adamant positions. Here are two rules I use in this respect, whereby it must of course be remembered that rules are not laws:

- One person = one short sentence!
- Do not subtract or break up—add to!

  For example:
  Not like this

Therapist: Once upon a time there was . .

Member A:. . . a huge desert. . .

Member B . . . no, not that. . . a beautiful field. . .

Member C:. . . oh no, not that . . . a big lake. . .

but rather

Therapist: Once upon a time there was . . .

Member A:. . . a huge desert. . .

Member B . . . behind which lay a beautiful field . . .

Member C:. . . that bordered on a big lake . . .

(A colleague of mine once commented on this: "Oh, I see, nothing repressive, but rather appositive—additional, supportive—growth.")

A good example of joint fairy-tale invention comes from a weekend seminar in continuing education I conducted in a Moreno Institute, which consisted of six three-hour sessions. The 16 participants (six men and ten women) and I had decided to use the fourth three-hour session to write a fairy tale together. Much like in group guided affective therapy, the participants were given the suggestion to lie in a star-formed pattern on the floor or on a blanket, with their heads in the middle and their legs to the outside. This particular group, however, chose to sit on chairs in a circle. Before we began, I requested that everyone speak clearly and loud enough so that I could take notes in telegram style which would be used later as a basis for working through the story.

I should mention that the following text was written down in complete sentences only later, and that the group participants decided who had said what. A number of different titles were suggested. Most popular were "Helpful Things," "The Captive Girl," and "The Hard Times of a Prince." The group in the end chose the last suggestion, since the king's son—the Prince—was most like a fairy-tale hero.

Leader: Long, long ago . . .

HD: . . . there was a dilapidated old castle in the far reaches of a deep forest . . .

B: . . . where lived an old woman and her dog . . .

BR: . . . for whom there were only two small rooms . . .

HE: . . . and a young girl lived with them . . .

P: Only very few people came to this area, and when they did come, they usually avoided it.

I: The evening bird sang in a tree . . .

H: . . . and the vegetation there was very different . . .

A: There was a wonderful flower, whose name was unknown but to few.

E: The animals avoided going near the castle, it was very quiet there.

HD: And there was also a cave there . . .

I: . . . and one could hear a gurgling from out of the earth.

HEL: Once a year a young man came to deliver goods . . .

H: . . . but he didn't talk about this . . .

F: . . . for he was dumb . . .

P: . . . and blind . . . (giggling)

W: The king of the castle thus told him to write down his experiences.

A: And so it became known that a young girl lived there.

B: The Prince then left to go to the castle.

P: He didn't listen to the warnings.

HE: On the roadside he found three plants . . .

BR: . . . he thought it would be easier . . .

W: . . . one was called "light flower". . .

A: . . . and it became a bright bird.

P: The second one was called wolfweed, and whoever ate of it became a wolf for a day.

HD: He ate of it . . .

I: . . . no, not yet!

HD: And he asked the bird . . .

A: . . . who understood him . . .

HE: The meaning of the third flower . . . a magic flower . . .

W: The Prince neared the castle . . .

AD: . . . the chains rattled, and three bears stood before the entrance.

HEL: The old woman had closed and locked all the doors and windows.

HE: From her room in the tower the girl looked down . . . .salind!58ë#IHD: . . . a dwavedtdh

HD: . . . and waved to him . . .

P: But the window panes were so cloudy, she thought she might have just imagined seeing him.

B: He came nearer. The raven on the roof shrieked: "Beware of the third flower!" . . .

R: The old woman came out of the house, and the young Prince rushed upon her . . .

I: . . . but she jumped to the side and disappeared.

J: It became dark . . . and strange birds appeared . . .

HE: . . . and the bears ducked and cowered . . .

W: . . . they had torsos of steel . . .

F: The Prince was terrified . . . and fled to the cave.

IT: Thank God he had the three flowers . . .

AG: . . . he ate of the wolfweed . . . the bears became afraid and receded.

HE: A tunnel led from the cave into the castle . . .

A: . . . it ended in a great round room with many doors.

W: The Prince was in despair: The bears were still to be defeated and there was no way out.

AD: The entrance to the round room was now closed off and all doors, as well.

A: . . . one like the other . . .

W: He desperately began to try all the doors . . .

AG: . . . there was a noise . . .

F: . . . then he saw skeletons and skulls . . .

HE: One of the doors had a handle. It lead to winding stairs . . .

BR: . . . that went down, however . . .

AG: . . . the noise became louder . . .

W: . . . people with swords of bone came toward him . . .

AG: . . . but this did not frighten him, for . . .

F: . . . he was a wolf!

A: Deeper and deeper he ran, and came finally upon a river. A huge fish sprang up . . .

W: . . . and said: "You will be delivered . . . you will find a way out, if you bathe in the river."

AG: The wolf said: "Well, I can swim" . . .

I: . . . and he jumped into the river and floated along.

HD: He had taken hold of the fish . . .

HE: . . . on the back of the fish he glided through underground passageways, and exited in the well in the castle's middle.

I: The Prince fell . . . the third flower was hard as a knife and he cut himself . . .

BR: . . . and his blood dripped onto the threshold of the tower door . . .

HE: . . . the tower door sprang open ..

AG: . . . and stairs led up the tower (hurried)

A: He dragged himself up with the last ounces of energy he had . . .

AG: . . . came into the room at the top . . .

HE: . . . and embraced the girl!

AG: In a thunderclap the old woman and the castle disappeared.

HE: "Come to my castle," the Prince said to the girl . . .

Leader: . . . and they lived happily ever after.

Subsequently, we went through the text slowly and exactly, removed mistakes, and studied false interpretations arising from misunderstandings and slips of the tongue. The literal text of each individual participant was used even when the other participants claimed that something else had in fact been said. In all psychotherapeutic forms, it is important that the clients have the feeling that even their slightest and strangest statement will be taken seriously, and thus that their integrity is respected. Such a feeling furthers openness more quickly and surely than appealing to the clients' reason or reminding them of rules or the prerequisites of the therapy: Only then can patients or course participants see their own contributions, and all have the opportunity to experience just how and in what direction they influenced the developing fairy tale.

Of course, it is also important to keep in mind not only the character and personality of the individual participants, but also the relevant group situation and group dynamics, any transference relationships to individual members and to the leader as well as concrete interventions on the part of the others. For example, when AG (see above) hurriedly says: "stairs led up the tower," it should be remembered that BR had, immediately after mention of the winding stairs, already said that they "went down, however." To take the hurriedness of the participants as a character trait would be both false and irresponsible.

Similar caution must be taken in the judgment of the amount of activity of any individual. That someone makes only one contribution need not point to little feeling of participation, but may express the person's reluctance to being exposed, or a feeling of complete satisfaction with the one comment—or the feeling that one's ideas just don't fit into the story. R (mid-story) felt her idea had been rejected; she had wanted a direct confrontation between the old woman and the Prince. So when I let the old woman jump back immediately and disappear, R stopped contributing. J, too, felt that his suggestion of darkness and the strange birds had not been accepted. IT, on the other hand, was satisfied by her reminder of the presence of the three flowers, and indeed she was generally satisfied with the rest of the tale.

One should also reflect on the repeated contributions of some members before drawing conclusions. Viewing all the different possible interpretations first is better than coming to a hard and fast opinion all too soon. Take the time to follow the exact sequence of experience of the individual members—if the person is willing to go along.

For example, P described his feelings as follows: "I wanted to introduce something dangerous. I was so mad that the delivery boy popped up that I blurted out that he was blind." (He laughs contentedly, somewhat sheepishly.) "That the warnings didn't stop the Prince was meant to illustrate his determinedness. I didn't like the light flower, it was too noble and pompous for me, and then the wolfweed occurred to me. I wanted him to be dangerous—that he too could become dangerous. But I didn't like much the girl's attention, which didn't seem realistic to me. Then I had the idea that the girl was only the old woman's decoy— that the Prince was to be duped!" P spoke then of his own distrust of direct attention of women toward men, and of his desire—at an appropriate moment—to get to know "the wolf" in himself.

In contrast to P, whose contributions stopped about halfway through, AG set in only in the second half of the story. P was, of course, pleased that AG let the Prince eat of the wolfweed; he admired and envied her that she let things get very dangerous; and he liked her brave wolf, who could swim. But he especially liked how she had the Prince go quickly up the stairs—and how quickly he brought the whole matter to an end.

AG, however, noted that she often had difficulties acting quickly enough. In order to become active herself, she had needed the cry of the raven, the strange birds, the steeled breasts of the bears (who, in her opinion, had ducked only to begin an attack), and finally the shock of the Prince. But, she said, when she does

Name	No. of Lines	Entry	Exit	Roles and Influence
Mr. HD	6	begin.		initiator, introduced activity
Ms. B	3	begin.	middle	introduced persons
Mr. BR	4	begin.		held to reality, then made path difficult
Ms. HE	10	begin.		introduced girl, helpful, contributed to happy end
Mr. P	5	begin.	middle	avoidance behavior, then warnings and introduction of wolfweed; distrust of women
Ms. I	6	begin.		raised tension, rejection of quick solutions
Ms. H	2	begin.	halfway	magical content and silence when "normal love story" began
Ms. A	8	begin.		supernatural, fairy-tale events, metamorphoses
Ms. F	5	begin.		quiet and mute, clarity, shock
Mr. HEL	2	begin.	middle	banal-realistic events; when it became too "magic-filled," exited
Mr. W	7	halfway		clarity, exact description; after despair introduction of hope
Ms. AD	2	middle	middle	threat and hopelessness
Ms. R	1	middle	middle	attempt at confrontation
Mr. J	1	middle	middle	dark, strange things
Ms. IT	1	middle	middle	reminded of possibility
Ms. AG	8	middle		forward-driving, efficiency, happy end

begin something, she carries it through to the end. She had often been told that she always had to have her own way, and once someone had noted that her apparent passivity at the beginning only deceived others in their assessment of her willpower and ability to assert herself. That comment made her feel misunderstood, as that was not her intention.

Space here does not allow us to study the experience of each individual participant in depth. (Some later wrote down their own contributions and discussed them with other members of the group.) A list in table form covering the members in the order of their appearance, their sex, the number of contributions, the type of influence they had, and the time of their entrance or exit must suffice. The listings under "Roles and Influence" are, of course, not complete, but serve rather to promote a study of the development of the story and the "game" that went on between the participants. Finally, this column lists the individual behaviors (the "pushers," the "thinkers," the "realists"). Some introduce strange, supernatural things—horrible things even. Often there is also a joker present who turns the whole fairy tale into a farce.

My experience of the last 20 years has shown that participants tend to slip into roles that are typical for them, thus exerting a very particular influence on the developing tale. The differences among the individual participants can be very large, depending on the flexibility of the individuals. As with dreams, the extent of (false) positions and of inhibitions is decisive [47, 48]. A domineering person will also domineer in fairy-tale telling, a helpful person will be helpful, etc. With very severely neurotic persons, a few actions may suffice to make reliable conclusions, though it would be erroneous if not dangerous to adhere to the theory of personality and neurosis development: Only within the context of the actual situation, the life history, and the ideas of the individual person can one make exact statements about the storyteller (cf. [44] on personality-specific matters; and [45] on the influence of the personality structure of the therapist on the course of therapy). In a previous book of mine [11] I touched on these points concerning the various influences in so-called creative work methods.

All the above-mentioned factors taken together contribute to whether the fairy tale has symbolic and magical content, and whether metamorphic phenomena are possible. In addition, there are the factors of group size, setting, and other therapeutic conditions. On the part of the therapists, the extent of their receptiveness toward fairy-tale content and their own fear threshold during the very creation of the fairy-tale play a large role. Very active therapists should try to keep their own tendencies to proceed forcefully toward ever deeper levels in check, as otherwise the functional ability of the group could be impaired.

Imagining, Drawing, Painting, and Modeling Fairy-Tale Scenes

These methods of using fairy tales therapeutically have one thing in common: their graphic nature. When, in a picture, figures and things are present that do not really exist, we should consider the possibility of metaphoric content. Yet we cannot know whether the deviation from reality is a sign, an allegory, or a symbol—or whether it is simple the result of insufficient skills. With imaginings we should consider not only deficient practice, but the limits of the fantasy of the storyteller as well; with drawing, painting, and modeling the extent of manual dexterity should be taken into account. One client, speaking about the difficulty of putting an idea into a drawing or painting, said the following: "Not only are my hands too clumsy and untrained, somehow the whole thing is different when I put it onto paper." With modeling it is easier for beginners to keep trying on the same piece, with the help of the failures as it were, to produce sculptures that fit their ideas reasonably well.

Mythological, Magical, and Fairy-Tale Content in Inner Scenes

The occurrence and dealings with supernatural figures and animated objects are expressly mentioned and described in Guided Affective Imagery [35]. Since, on the subject level, we are dealing with representatives of the person's own character makeup, it is important not to injure or destroy them. Thus, in the beginner's stage, nourishing, accepting, and (if possible) liking the person are important; integration can be strived for later. In an emergency, the supernatural figure should be banned. Make friendly contact and try to start a dialog. Take spontaneous beginnings and minor magical details seriously, even (or especially) if they occur in a well-known landscape grounded in reality.

Here the vision of one participant of a seminar on the theme of "Sagas and Fairy Tales in Guided Mental Imagery":

> I am walking on a narrow road in mountainous woods—like the upper one on that mountain there (points out the window to a nearby mountainside)—and the valley is to my right. The trees are very thick, mostly firs and pines. Sometimes I can see all the way down. But there are no houses there (not like the local situation in which a part of the city stretches through the whole valley) . . . The air is brisk and the sun is shining, like in the early morning. Al of a sudden, directly ahead on my path, I see a very *strange tree*. It doesn't fit into the landscape at all: It's not very big, maybe 2 to 2 1/2 meters tall, and has a very short trunk from which four or five main branches emanate at a single point; these have only very few smaller branches. At the ends of these small branches hang large, limp, thick, almost fleshy leaves. With

three or four points, like these (draws a leaf with the right hand in the air). And it's strange—directly at the point where the leaf joins the stem there's these oval things, almost like heads.

Leader: Look closer.

Participant: Yes, they are heads. The one across from me is larger, about the size of a tennis ball, but oval. And there are eye slits and a lipless mouth and small nostrils . . . like this (models them with both hands in the air, much like children show others a "moon face"). I want to touch the leaves and the balls . . . no, they now look more like large figs perched on top; but I can't bring myself to feel them.

Leader: What else would you like to do?

Participant: Well, I could . . . (speaks as though talking with another person) ask him.

There is a short pause in which the course leader, in a voice reflecting both positive support and questioning, says "Mmmm."

Participant (no longer with a clear, descriptive, sober voice, but rather in with soft tones, in a mixture of respect, personal engagement, and not wanting to bother): Can you tell me something? . . . Now he's opening the eyelids a bit . . . he now looks like an wise, old Chinese man.

Participant (speaking for the head): What do you want?

Participant: I don't really know . . . but you look so old and wise—don't you want to tell me something?

Participant (as head): . . .

Participant: He's looking at me quietly, but not saying a thing.

Leader: And his facial expression?

Participant: Calm and peaceful, as if from afar . . . But he's looking at me as a whole, not just into my eyes . . . I'd like to stay here a while.

Leader: OK.

Participant: I'll just stay here . . . I feel very calm myself . . . (after a while) . . . now the eyelids are closed . . . I can barely see the mouth and eyelids any more . . . it is again like the other egg-shaped . . . things.

Leader: Maybe you could take the peacefulness with you.

Participant: Yes, . . . and maybe return sometime.

Leader: Then keep the peacefulness and take with you as well—if you like—the picture of yourself being observed as a whole . . .

At this point the "journey through the inner landscape" was concluded in the usual manner. One section of the later discussion was in my opinion particularly important:

Participant (still very moved): He looked at me very peacefully, full of wisdom somehow . . . but . . . (sad and somewhat disappointed) he didn't say anything . . .

Leader: And he looked at you as a whole being.

Participant: Yes, he only looked at me peacefully, and as a whole being.

Leader (slowly and deliberately): "Only"? . . . as a whole being?!

Participant (after a pause): . . . yes, yes! He told me something with that . . . no, he gave me something . . . seeing me peacefully as a whole being.

Leader (does not give a supportive "Well, that is something you can take with you" or "There you've received something very valuable," but gives only a warm reaction): Hmmm.

With such deeply seated, magical, and symbolic experiences, it is a question of how much can or should be worked through verbally. If something has clearly touched the client and has been accepted by the client, I often let the experience stand as it is, leaving the client to his/her own feelings, and say nothing for my part until the client begins again. It is important to notice whether the client sticks to the theme at hand, or whether (and how) the theme is subsumed, directly or indirectly, into the subsequent conversation. Sometimes it recurs in a dream, a picture, or even in the actions of the client in the real world. As important as it is to help the person to see clearly and to study—to enrich and magnify—the visual material, it is just as important not to "talk away" the actual experience: It might then be shifted from the direct feelings to more rational levels.

It may be just chance that the above-mentioned participant saw only a head and not a complete figure. Heyer [22] said in this regard, however: "Chance is what happens." The participant was a good, realistic, and, as one can see in his description, an exact observer. He looked with his own eyes in his own head and saw a "head" and "wise eyes" that did not simply observe him, but embraced his entity, as it were, in a knowing, peaceful, even soulful glance. I avoided having the participant see the episode from a rational point of view; rather, I wanted to leave him to his own feelings in order that he might have a true *experience* and not a mere intellectual understanding.

In the section above on "Reading Fairy Tales Aloud" (p. 16), I mentioned that one can, in fact, stimulate graphic imagery in listeners, be they clients or training candidates. The same is true, of course, when inventing fairy tales and other mythological stories. For example, during the development of the fairy tale "The Hard Times of a Prince" (pp. 44), the majority of the group sat with closed eyes and imagined the scene. And even after the authors of the individual sections had been determined, most participants held their eyes closed during the rereading of the entire fairy tale. Shutting out optical disturbances is a spontaneous reaction well known from the concert hall: It allows concentration on acoustical events. And it is no secret that the eyelids seem to close of themselves in moments of intensive emotional experience. So it is certainly understandable that, when trying to concentrate on one's own inner images and fantasies, one wants to shut out external optical disturbances. In Guided Affective Imagery, it is absolutely necessary that the inner images arising be described in detail, as otherwise the therapist cannot fully understand the client's image. And the therapist, at least during training, should not try to form his or her own image, but rather follow the images of the client and if necessary assist. If the therapist's own images nevertheless become too strong, it is of utmost importance that the *difference* between the client's and the therapist's images be studied in order to avoid misunderstandings and false interventions as a result.

Högberg [23] pointed out something very important concerning graphic images of fairy tales and similar texts: The descriptive language used both in fairy tales and in myths and sagas is often very meager indeed and with few details—and it is this very fact that allows readers (or even better: listeners with their eyes closed) to experience their own images.

For example:

"A mermaid came up out of the ocean and neared. . ."—before continuing, the reader should sit down for a minute or two, close the eyes and envision mermaids, the ocean and the mermaid's actions, maybe even draw this scene. Then compare the images one has with those of the following, extensive, very poetic and yet *definitive* description:

"A mermaid with long blond hair interlaced with sea grass and with beautiful blue eyes set in a delicate face emerged from the glass-like ocean. Her body was white as alabaster and her tender breasts shone in the sun. As she neared dolphin-like, one could see, covered with glittering scales, her green tail, which at its end was split into two tail fins."

The more precise and detailed a description is, the less room it leaves for one's own imagination. It is my observation in the Anglo-American part of the world and in people who have seen Disney movies repeatedly that the movement and expressions displayed so well in these films are copied, making one's own graphic fantasies less potent. This is all the more important because the specific embodiment of a fairy-tale figure often reduces the credibility of the conflicts present in the tale. For example, it appears absurd to us that the mirror in Disney's *Snow White and the Seven Dwarfs* should announce to the queen, who is certainly an impressive figure, but even in her less terrifying moments hardly a *beautiful* stepmother: "You're the fairest here, but. . ." etc. With this the mirror loses a part of its magical function as teller of truth.

Thus, if we are interested in working with the imaginative ideas of our clients therapeutically, we would do well to leave them a lot of space.

The step from visual imagination to physical production of our images is then a very short one indeed.

Drawing, Painting, and Modeling Fairy-Tale Scenes and Figures

Before going into the different work methods, I would like to make a few comments on how to make passing the threshold from imagination to concrete expression easier. When trying to animate a group to creative activities, one should speak not of "drawings" and "paintings," but rather of "sketches." I try to avoid all statements that might give the clients cause to reply: "I can't do that," "I was always bad at that in school," "I'm just not talented enough for that," "It's not my thing," etc. If, while describing something particular, a client begins to draw or form the image in the air with the hands, it may be a good opportunity for the therapist to say: "You're sketching/forming . . . and apparently you have a very good idea—a very graphic idea—of what it looks like. Maybe sketching it would help to show better what you mean." The latter part of this suggestion may be varied to correspond to the predominant parts of the personality structure of the respective client. For example, for someone who generally tends toward depression, one might say: ". . . a sketch might help me to see it as you do"; with a compulsive: ". . . a sketch might better show what you see, so that we can get a very detailed picture of things for our further work"; for a hysterically structured client: ". . . a small sketch could relax you . . . (and should it fit the method of treatment, one could add:) I'm curious to see what results"; with a predominantly schizoid person (intentional or early disturbed), it is important to recognize his/her autonomy: ". . . a sketch could help to gain respect for *your* images."

The phrases listed above are meant to reach patients by using the language closest to their experience. Every therapist, however, must find different means and ways of approaching different clients without it appearing condescending, staged, or forced. And this also means that therapists must take their own character structure into account [45].

Understanding a client's images is sometimes made easier when the therapist approaches the task concretely and makes a sketch of his/her own and then shows it to the client with the words: "Is that correct? Have I understood things correctly?" This may then cause the client to complete or change the picture and thus become the active person. If the therapist succeeds in having the client experience the relationship between the formed image and his/her own inner world, then the client's motivation to continue drawing, painting, and modeling in the future will be raised considerably. On the other hand, if the result is felt to be foreign, disparate, or irrelevant, further attempts will not follow. The therapist then risks interpreting such behavior as resistance on the part of the client—causing a turn toward an (in this case unnecessary) resistance analysis instead of concentrating on more creative and understanding cooperation.

Some clients find it easier to first draw and model alone. This behavior should be supported, at least at the beginning. It is important that the presence of the therapist be expressly desired by the client. Obviously, the therapist can get a better picture of the client's activity when present during the creative process; this saves the client the effort of explaining the picture/sculpture later, leading to deeper and better founded insight into the relationship between the client's creative actions and his/her personality.

Creativity is fostered when various drawing and painting utensils are present so that each patient can choose a pencil or brush as well as paper suitable to the respective task. In addition to making statements through their choices, clients are usually pleased at the very fact of *having a choice* and not being forced to conform. Persons with less ability to decide for themselves may of course always be made offers that are judged to correspond best to their personality.

More details on beginning creative therapy and dealing with the creative experience of patients may be found in an earlier book of mine (11); I do not go further into it here, as it would go beyond the scope of this book and its main subject: fairy tales.

Here, however, a few examples to show the variety of possibilities:

• *Sketching, painting, and sculpturing after the reading of a fairy tale*

This can be done directly after the therapist has read a text (see also page 19) or after the group has decided on a fairy tale of direct relevance to the group theme. The following is a description of what happened after the fairy tale *Rapunzel* [19] was read aloud:

In a course for continuing education this fairy tale was chosen because the group wanted a tale in which neither a male nor female played the leading role. As well, it should deal neither with siblings (*Hansel and Gretel, Little Brother and Sister,* etc.) nor with lovers (e.g., *Jorinda and Joringel*). Because it took such a long time to choose the proper tale, and because the person reading it went very slowly, with great feeling and expression, there remained little time for discussion: The group leader suggested delaying the acting-out of the tale until the next day; in the meantime, the members of the group should draw simple sketches or pictures of one or two scenes or figures and bring them along. One should choose a detail or a section of the tale that had been especially impressive or touching.

To the surprise of all, every participant brought along a sketch or a picture. (One colleague was very angry with herself that she had left her picture at home.) The sketches were laid out, and each participant was allowed to comment upon them as desired. The group leader made the following suggestions:

- Describe, but do not interpret.

- The creator may listen to what the others have to say. What is seen, however, has most definitely to do with the observer—and *maybe* with the creator. No one should take to heart something that is foreign or unfitting to him or her.

- Not only the theme and general impression of the sketch, but also details, such as thickness of stroke and pressure points, should be considered.

- How often certain themes occur can be indicative of the group situation, though it may also have to do with the individuals themselves.

(I personally would not introduce the last comment in a group of patients, as this might cause them to turn from their own experience to a more intellectual view of the matter. In the above-mentioned, highly motivated group of therapists, however, such caution was not necessary.)

The group, including the group leader, consisted of nine women and six men. Unfortunately, not all pictures can be considered here. (Note: The pictures mentioned in the text have been gathered and printed at the middle of the book.) One may clearly see that the females in the group frequently chose the appeal of the forbidden (Figure I), the lust for rapunzel (= lamb's lettuce; in early translations called radishes) (Figure 1a), and experiences of loss (Figure 1b: the child is taken away; Figure 1c: the pigtail is cut off). Concerning Figure I one should mention that the painter is situated in front of the (blue) barrier below, from which vantage point the forbidden things in their bright colors appear very attractive and inviting. The graphic depictions in the sketches of Figure 1a—c startled the group, whereby it is important to note that both the creator and her work as well as the shock the group experienced were accepted by the group leader. Here it suffices to say: Clear and unfettered messages can really be shocking. Yet because of their clarity of expression, they are particularly useful in gaining insight—and are thus to be welcomed.

One female colleague chose the tower theme and drew the window such that many other participants overlooked it completely. It was also the only depiction of the tower which did not include hair. It is surrounded at the bottom by thick shrubbery (Figure IIa). This led to comparisons with the story of *Sleeping Beauty.*

Only one of the six men in the group took up the theme of the lust of the woman for rapunzel, and this only as a facet of power. In two drawings (Figure 2), he depicted the man (this at least was the impression of another male participant) as a "sausage with legs." For the creator himself "Power I" depicts the lust of the woman for rapunzel and her order to procure it; "Power II" a scene in which the sorceress is ruling over her rapunzel and gives the man the ultimatum. One female participant was interested particularly in the sorceress' dark hat; a male participant thought the head depicted in "Power I" looked as though it had received many a blow with the frying pan. Another participant thought the drawing showed only the lower part of the body, and that the nose was in fact a penis. At this juncture several possibilities were discussed as to how certain aspects of the woman may be experienced as threatening and dominating. Further, it was noted that the man has feet but neither arms nor hands—and thus cannot take any action. The latter corresponded to the experience of the creator, who had been impressed by the powerlessness of the man. A female participant said with a smile: "At home, with his wife, he looks a lot smaller than when beside the sorceress." "Yes, but in the latter there is a wall between them, and it is bigger than the table," another participant mentioned.

One man was impressed by the final scene and drew the persons involved as squiggles in the desert (Figure 3). The distance from the bottom of the page to the "Prince" symbolizes, he said, the long journey through the desert; the Prince has already regained his sight in the drawing and is now confronted with the fact that Rapunzel and the twins belong together. The small opening toward the Prince in the squiggle representing Rapunzel was compared by other participants to the closed state of that representing the Prince. The colleague who had been so concerned with "power" saw here too the connection: three against one. One female participant later said that this picture had helped her—"after all these years"—to understand the situation of her own father who had once returned from a long time as a prisoner of war.

Another man in the group was fascinated by the passage in which the Prince was blinded by the thorns after his jump from the tower, and how he later regained his sight through Rapunzel's tears (Figure IIIa and b). The long, golden hair was important to him; and when he drew his picture, he showed it still hanging from the tower where the Prince was lying. One female participant had the fantasy that the tower with the golden hair was only an inner representation of the

Prince. Some group members then discussed the difference in the relationships among the persons in the story when comparing Figure IIIb with Figure 3. One female participant thought that Rapunzel's children were depicted in their correct ages in Figure IIIb, but that the maternal connection in Figure 3 was extremely umbilical. To which another participant replied that this is certainly understandable in the light of the situation of isolation shown.

Three of the six males drew only the tower, the hair, and the Prince, albeit with interesting differences in their choices of plot and time. In Figure IIb, the well-braided tresses are emphasized; the Prince is present only in the tip of his hat peeking out from behind a tree on the left side, with a little bit of profile. The creator wanted to capture the moment in which the prince spies Rapunzel's tresses and is enraptured by them. Rapunzel's head can also be seen in the window.

In another drawing (Figure IIc) the prince has a crown on his head and has just jumped from his barebacked horse to the long braid, which he is holding in one hand. The group's interpretations ran the gamut from seeing great dexterity and strength (be it in reality or in fantasy) to fearing that the Prince would promptly fall down.

The creator of Figure IV did not reveal anything. The opinion of the group members was that in this depiction the Prince had progressed a good part up the tower (though it is not known how far he had already climbed); he appears to see his goal clearly and to be about to reach it. Further, the prince and his crown are depicted very distinctly, and the tower appears particularly imposing.

Further discussions centered around the fact that four of the six men were touched or fascinated by the motifs of the tower and the hair/braid. This led to a discussion about the height of the tower relative to the respective creator's "visions of achievability." The height of the towers in Figures IIc and IV cannot be accurately judged, as in the former the upper part, in the latter the lower part are not shown. Both, however, would surely be between 6 and 7 meters (20–23 ft.). The only tower drawn by a woman (Figure IIa), on the other hand, was not very high, perhaps 3 to 4 meters (10–13 ft.) to the lower edge of the window—yet there were no tresses and the window had bars on it.

The material of this group concerning the tower—this is my opinion, in any case—does not warrant a single symbolic interpretation. Even a very broad view of the phallus symbol, for example, would not comprise the aspects of protection and enclosure. And, on the other hand, pursuing exclusively the aspect of being locked up would ignore the fact that Rapunzel is at the top of a *tower*: She certainly could have been detained more safely and less conspicuously in a dungeon or a cave.

For our psychotherapeutic work, it is decisive to determine what a particular tale occasions in clients and what it means to them—not what it has to say when viewed from various theoretical angles. Of course, it does expedite things if the therapist is acquainted with various ways of interpretation, which can then serve as a background for the individual form of experience and interpretation of the respective client.

A major task for the group leader/therapist is to see to it that the capabilities of the group as a whole are not overtaxed, and that the ego strength of the individual participants are neither under- nor overestimated. Introductory information can certainly help matters, but it cannot relieve the therapist of the task of avoiding or attenuating unnecessary pressures and hurt feelings as well as of ensuring that work in the group is constructive and understanding. Direct destructive tendencies are often less difficult to deal with than are subtle—and often unconscious—"pointed" statements.

The use of creative work methods mobilizes forces through playful, constructive activities; it brings forth conflicts; it causes cathartic reactions; and it releases rich experiental material [11]. One can never say for sure whether a remark or a description will be well received or whether it will touch a nerve in the client or group participant. With hurt and touched feelings it is as mentioned above: Directly or even profusely expressed, they are less problematic than when subtle or subliminal. Withdrawnness, absentmindedness may reflect intense inner activity and should not always be remarked upon immediately. Yet the same behavior may also be a sign of an inner retreat because of a hurt feeling. Sometimes, in situations in which two or three participants seem to be more in themselves than in the group, I say before ending the session: "I would like to take a second or two for those who have been silent up to now. If you would rather keep things to yourself or deal with things alone, that is certainly acceptable." The final sentence is meant to avoid unnecessary group or therapist pressure. If there is no reply, after a few seconds—before a momentous silence can develop—I end the group session.

In short-term encounter groups, such as at congresses and meetings, it has proved useful to give the following information at the beginning:

- During the sessions say and contribute only as much as you can while retaining a good feeling.

- If something comes up in you which you cannot bring up in the group because of time limitations, I (or my co-therapist) are at your disposal for a short conversation alone.

There, at least hints may be given as to various possibilities for working through matters in the future.

I have repeatedly had the experience that short-term groups become progressively more frank if one does not actively try to promote such behavior. With continuous long-term groups, of course, it is not advised to disturb or hinder the development and depth of the group work by having individual conversations with the therapist.

• *Graphic depictions after a fairy-tale performance*

Here, of course, there are also several possibilities. Some clients may bring along pictures on their own of a particular scene that fascinated them during the performance. In therapies in which the painting of inner scenes is furthered or even an integral part [7, 9, 22, 27, 28, 29, 50], such behavior will occur more often than in strictly conversational therapies. The opposite to the spontaneous production of pictures is the direct request: The client is given the task of drawing, painting, or molding a particular scene. For example, a female client who had suppressed all emotion while playing in *Cinderella* was asked by the group to paint the scene in which Cinderella cries over her mother's grave, thus causing the tree to grow. Here, the client received exact thematic instructions.

In the Psychosomatic Department of the University Medical Clinic in Freiburg, West Germany, it was once the custom that entrance to individual therapeutic sessions required a "ticket"—a dream, a picture, or an experience from psychodrama, motion therapy, or one of the internal get-togethers. Thus, creative activities were rewarded, albeit without influencing the content of the respective activity.

An example:

A 26-year-old, married female patient with a 6-year-old daughter had suffered from manifold and in part shifting symptoms since the birth of the child. In the order of their subjective severity the patient reported them as follows:

- frigidity and anorgasmy
- extreme, sudden headache
- spastic abdominal pains with nausea and dizziness
- dysmenorrhoe
- sleeping problems with increased sleep need
- back pains in the lumbar vertebral and sacral areas.

The pregnancy had been planned in order to escape home by having to get married. As an inpatient she was very helpful on the station and had difficulties saying no. When the roles for *Sleeping Beauty* were given out, she volunteered quickly to play the good twelfth fairy, who has the power to change the death curse of the uninvited thirteenth fairy into the 100-year sleep. Immediately after the presentation of the fairy tale, the patient noted during the discussion that it wouldn't matter at all if she herself were to sleep through the next 100 years.

The patient brought along the chalk drawing shown in Figure V to the next individual session. She said that after the fairy-tale performance she had thought intensively about her daughter, and that it was very important for her to spare her daughter such awful things. On the other hand, the daughter should also spend a lot of time in natural surroundings, thus her presence during every vacation—which bothered her husband. The picture is meant to depict the daughter outdoors and yet protected: see the garden gate and the fence with pergola. She said it was also important to her that the sun be shining and that a tree be present. The birds are meant to liven up everything—after all it's already a sad fact that the daughter is an only child. (But with her many ailments she hadn't dared to have another child.) The rosebush reflects the story of *Sleeping Beauty.* When asked whether anything else occurred to her, she said that the child was apparently pointing to something or perhaps wanted to have something.

Some of the details of the drawing caught the therapist's eye: The tree is missing its bottom most two limbs; the one bird is placed exactly above the child; the protective role of the fence for the child is not necessarily felt as such; it is at least questionable whether the garden gate can be opened or locked; the entire background is unclear; the sky is dark. Instead of encouraging the patient to expand on these, the therapist requested that she take the picture to the next session of the analytically oriented group, where she felt comfortable. Maybe many eyes could see more than those of patient and therapist.

Comments from the group included the following: "Oh, isn't she sweet, the little girl, and so full of life." "She looks younger than 6 years old." At this point, the other members guessed the age of the child to be from 3 to 5 years, with one judging 10 years. "The sun is shining, it's pretty." "But the sky is full of such threatening clouds." "The rosebush looks friendly and is stretching a branch over the child." "But above that there is this black bird . . . and if he . . . you know, the child gets it on the head" (laughter). "I like the tree . . . you took great effort painting the leaves." "The lower two branches are sawed off." "Two birds are approaching in flight." "I wonder what they are bringing with them . . . that reminds me of the three ravens that fly around the ship and warn faithful John." "I can't make out what the landscape behind the tree looks like."

These comments made the patient very thoughtful. She had only wanted to make the setting as friendly as possible for the child, and yet apparently a great deal of insecurity and maybe even threat was put into the picture. In further group sessions and psychodramas the patient was actively concerned with these different aspects and later mastered her life situation without major problems.

Now a further example of modeling after a fairy-tale presentation. I have chosen *Sleeping Beauty* on purpose in order to show how important it is to take personal fascination into account. Upon hearing from two people that they have the same favorite fairy tale, one cannot conclude anything about similarities between them or assume similar psychodynamics. Even if they both choose the same part of the story, they can be experiencing it very differently. One person may enjoy the thought of the 100-year sleep, another may judge the imposed immobility as a severe punishment.

During a weekend seminar on fairy-tale drama, a female participant was particularly struck by the following passage from *Sleeping Beauty*: ". . . and so it happened that on the day of the child's 15th birthday the king and the queen were not at home and the girl was alone in the castle. So she went everywhere, looked in every room and closet as she desired, and finally came upon an old tower. She climbed the winding stairs and arrived at a small door . . ."

It was the inspection of the castle, the inquisitiveness and initiative of Sleeping Beauty which fascinated the participant. She told the woman playing Sleeping Beauty: "If I were you I would have roamed much longer through the castle and had a good look at everything—I would have looked in every chest and trunk and searched through every cabinet." Later in the session she viewed the trip through the castle on a subjective level by looking at it as a picture of herself getting to know her own inner life—the rooms and corners of her own personality.

Later I received from this woman a modeled castle (the *Sleeping Beauty* castle?) shown in Figures 4a and 4b which she had formed of clay and had baked. It was important to her that there be different types of towers and an oriel; there were many special rooms for special occasions. And particularly important was that the gate always be open, at least slightly: She did not want a golden cage.

This castle stood for many years, unobtrusive yet quite visible, among other items in a cabinet in my consulting room. Of all my patients only one, a 28-year-old woman, was extremely moved by the castle. She was in a phase in which she, after many failures at mastering external reality, was turning to her "inner reality." She asked if she could look at it more closely, to which I agreed. She took it carefully in her hands, turned it over and studied it from all sides. She was especially fascinated upon turning it over to discover that all the towers were hollow from the inside and could thus be reached. I told her the story of how the castle had come to be and how it had to do with the passage in the story of *Sleeping Beauty*—and that the most important thing to the patient who had modeled the castle was the gate being left ajar. Here, she picked up the thread: "Well, sure, so that you can go in and out. But I personally would also want to be able to lock the gate, should someone come who shouldn't enter."

In following sessions the patient returned repeatedly to the modeled castle. She thought her way into various rooms. If she wanted to look out over the land peacefully, she preferred being in the highest room of the highest tower; if she were looking for guests coming to a festivity in the large hall, she went to the tower above the gate; if she were sad, she would retreat to the small room in the small tower above the addition (see Figure 4b). These conversations about the castle helped her to explore her own inner realms more thoroughly and deepened considerably the communication between the different parts of her personality, which previously had been isolated from each other and in fact had impeded each other.

These two women show, despite certain similarities in their experience, considerable differences. For the first, the participant in the course, it was a look back at an important phase of her childhood. For the latter patient it was a station on her path to self-discovery.

• *Group creations*

If we do not define the term fairy tale too narrowly, allowing for supernatural wishes and fantastic ideas, we have a wide range of possibilities here. For example, the graphic presentation of a fairy tale or a scene thereof and the modeling of an important figure from it by the entire group. Or the sketching of passages that have personally affected the clients (see above p. 55). And when working with masks [41, 43], much supernatural content may enter which allows insight into personality depths of the creator otherwise difficult to reach. Often the very character of the mask is a good sign for the meaning and the possible individuation of the *persona* of the client. On the other hand, the changes in expression a mask experiences, depending on the person wearing it, clearly show how susceptible it is to influences from within. The persona, the mask, the facade— terms I regard in separate senses, as they do not indicate the same thing—all these develop as conjunctions of inner wishes and necessities and external circumstances. Thus, it is not only unnecessary, but also damaging to ongoing therapy to dismiss a particular behavior as being a facade or foreign to the client's personality. For in the façade or mask often lie the "inner roots"—and a respectful and understanding attitude toward them may allow a look at what lies beneath. This, by the way, also corresponds to Freud's suggestion [15] to start with the surface presented, something that is valid today, too, if one is striving to offer clients an understanding of and a feeling for the connections between their inner workings and their behavior in external reality.

A number of suggestions from family therapy are interesting in this connection. When comparing a client's real family with the ideal family, one often finds that the latter contains surreal or magical images. It is very important to become aware of these even if a realization of such a family is neither possible nor desirable. The indicative value, however, is very high.

A study of *The Family as Animals* [18] for therapeutic purposes is also possible in groups. This method offers not only graphic and allegorical means of expression, but supernatural and fairy-tale-like themes and details as well. The same is true for similar methods, for example, the family as plants, as pieces of furniture, as musical instruments, etc. These have proved very useful if scruples exist about characterizing family members as animals.

In groups, the suggestion of painting together "My world—our world" sometimes leads to both allegorical and fairy-tale elements being brought forth. But if the therapist calls the theme "The real world—the fantasy world" (or fairy-tale world), supernatural contents abound. And the more or less clear transitions between the two can be the most fruitful.

In one particular group, the members decided to divide up the room on a large piece of paper hung on the wall (1.2 by 4 meters). On the left was the fairy-tale world, on the right the real world. In the middle, as delineation, there was a large lake (foreground) fed by a river (middle ground), which flowed from a canyon (background): The separation of the two areas was complete. The person who had suggested the separation and had succeeded in getting the others to agree was strictly against all attempts to close the gap, through a bridge or plank across the river, through a boat, through having ducks in the lake or whatever. He said: "They are two very different worlds, and they should not get mixed up." He himself stood most of the time exactly in the middle, nearly like a continuation of the border line. Yet all around him, and of course behind his back, the others traveled from one world to the other quite freely. He made no contribution to the fairy-tale world, thought it for the most part to be "silly" or "childish," and warned others not to "get lost" there.

In an encounter group concerned with the theme of "Inner images—outer images," after having lead some visual imaginations, I suggested that the participants form the world on a table, *exactly as they would like it and imagine it*, as material we used Plasticine. In a surprisingly short period of time a number of different reality-oriented and fantasy-oriented objects, in part containing supernatural elements, were formed, both alone and in groups (see Figure VI). A few comments here must suffice:

Note the completely realistic form of the block house and the relatively realistic blue female figure, whereas the brown "mother," with her cup-like form, is less a depiction than an allegorical, maybe even symbolic, statement. Feelings in the group associated with this figure ranged from acceptance, sheltering, protection, and care, to a being-there-for-the-child feeling that excludes attention to others. But as well tiredness, dejection, self-absorption, and lethargy were present in the figure for some members. The group worked together on the stream and the trees.

An approximately 50-year-old male participant formed the island in the rear all by himself; in its middle stood a "wonder tree" offering protection and nourishment. Once during the work session the boat of a colleague neared the island, and the man warned him of the coral riffs surrounding it: The white foam of the water was meant to show that the corals were directly under the water surface. When the "boatsman" followed his warning and kept his distance, the man gave him very useful information on how to sail by the island without danger. The independence he enjoyed, the autonomy, and the certainty of not being disturbed, made the chosen place for him a true "island of peace and tranquility."

These tendencies mirrored his behavior in the group: his stance at the edge of things, his warnings—friendly but determined—against any approaches and his effective thwarting of such, but also his distanced yet kind readiness to give advice from his own experience. The self-sufficiency and the subsistence shown through the tree, however, were new. Instead of trying to force him to make statements about himself, the group turned to his interests and hobbyies and eventually gained a deeper understanding for him and his way of life. Previously, it had been doubted whether he had the ability to be receptive to others at all; but now his warm interest appeared not only credible to most, some members had actually experienced it directly. His willingness to take part without meddling was seen as advantageous for his line of work, and it even occasioned comments such as the following: "I could put great trust in you" and "I would have liked to have had a father like you who gives me advice but without interfering."

I have chosen the above instead of some well-known fairy tale because it is usually more difficult to discern small indications of supernatural and symbolic content than to interpret completely fairy-tale-like stories. Peculiarities exhibited on a playful, fantastic level can be more easily accepted by others than those confronted in everyday reality: Tolerance for individuality appears to be greater when dealing with fantasies, pictures, and games. And as the situation in the case of the "islander" shows, this increased understanding can even be carried over into real situations.

The graphic depiction of fairy tales (or scenes thereof), myths, sagas, and other supernatural elements, I should also mention, always simultaneously represents a mental conception of the creator taking concrete form. This facilitates the confrontation with one's own inner representants and personality structure, which flow, so to speak, into the depiction and are expressed there.

The creative methods mentioned here and supported in part by examples do not, of course, represent all possible types. I think it is of utmost importance that the therapist ask him- or herself which type would be accepted at that particular moment by the client in question, and how this method can best serve the therapy. A deepening of the relationship between client and therapist results when new forms of cooperation develop corresponding to the personalities of the two parties. This, in turn, benefits *every* form of therapy according to the respective style, whether oriented toward learning new things, practicing new skills, giving relief, or imparting insight.

Performing Fairy Tales

Though various psychotherapeutic and especially psychoanalytic schools [2, 9, 13, 14, 17, 27] were concerned very early on with fairy tales, myths, and the supernatural, acting out fairy tales as a method in the therapy of adults appeared relatively late. Of course, there were some supernatural elements and techniques (e.g., Magic Shop) that did find their way into psychodrama [36, 39, 42]. To my knowledge the first to use the performance of fairy tales in the German-speaking countries as an indicated (group)therapeutic method in its own standing was Clauser [4] in the early 1950s. Enke and Maass [38] played a major role in the further development of this technique. I myself have experienced the effectiveness of acting out fairy tales since 1963 and have been able to test several different methods.

I would like to mention once again that the following depictions are meant only as examples for your inspiration. No technique should be *adopted* without considering whether it were better first *adapted*. Reasons for modifying a technique may lie in the individual client, in the theoretical background of the therapist, in the therapeutic goal, or certainly not the least in the circumstances present in the respective clinic or practice. In the following I illustrate various methods by means of examples.

In general, it can be said that the method chosen should be all the more structured, the lower the anxiety threshold and the smaller the coping capabilities of the participants. The length of the therapy or the length of the course is also important. Only when group cohesion is sound and a basic trust has been established can the group accept the increased stress created by having the greater amount of freedom found in unstructured methods. Active participation of the therapist, less suited to groups of patients, should be considered very carefully beforehand. The select use of trained "auxiliary egos" [36, 39], however, can be very valuable. In training and practice groups, for instance, the therapist and co-therapist can alternately take part in the performances. The less the participants need the therapist as projective object (in the sense of an extended transference neurosis), the wider the range of possibilities available to the therapist. The therapist may lose a halo but gains a better emotional contact to the others, as Knobloch [32] and others have observed. Some therapists are afraid that after taking part in performances they will no longer be taken seriously enough by the participants in their role as therapist. This may be true, yet in behavior-modifying and practical forms of therapy the exemplary behavior of the leader may in fact further matters. Thus, it remains up to the individual therapist to decide from case to case and from group to group, while still honoring the respective "house style," what to do and what to abstain from.

Figure 1a. Greed (see p. 56).

Figure 1b, c. Experience of loss (see p. 56).

Figure 2. Power (see p. 57).

Figure I. Temptation of the forbidden (see p. 56).

Figure II a,b,c. The tower from *Rapunzel* (see p. 57f.).

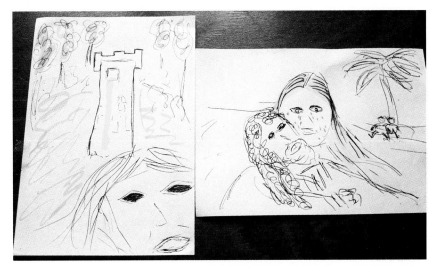

Figure IIIa. The tower (see p. 57).   **Figure IIIb.** Rapunzel's hair (see p. 57).

Figure 3. Rapunzel and the Prince in the desert (see p. 57).

Figure 4 a,b. Castle crafted after performance of *Sleeping Beauty* (see p. 62).

Figure 5. "Drought" before free fairy-tale improvisation (see p. 105).

Figure 6. The blind seer in the free fairy-tale improvisation (see pp. 95, 106).

Figure IV. Prince climbing up the
tower (see p. 58).

Figure V. Drawing made after performance of *Sleeping Beauty* (see p. 61).

Figure VI. Fantasy world; group creation in Plasticine (see p. 64).

Figure VII. Women's group with monk. Free fairy-tale improvisation (see p. 95).

Figure 7. Primitive horse (or moose-father) from free fairy-tale impro-visation (see p. 106).

Figure 8 a,b. Taking leave of the mother (left) and returning (right); from free fairy-tale improvisation (see pp. 107/108).

Folk, House, Maturation, and Literary Fairy Tales

In his work at the Psychosomatic Clinic of the Freiburg University Medical Center, Clauser [4] operated on the assumption that the acting-out of maturation tales by patients with functional somatic disorders following life crises would enhance their therapy. He also recognized and implemented the possibility of having new experiences while playing a fairy-tale role. Fairy-tale performance was one of the creative methods offered. Up to 1965, psychodrama [36, 39], pantomime (after Horetzky [25]), and fairy-tale performance alternated weekly on a three-part rotation system. Participation was voluntary, although a certain amount of pressure to attend was present, individual therapeutic conversations being available only to those having an "admission ticket" (see page 60). From 1966 onwards the style of therapy became more analytically oriented, so that reality-oriented psychodrama and role-playing came to be preferred. Sometimes, however, mostly in earlier patients taking up therapy again, desires for acting out fairy tales were expressed; these were often judged as escape, as fleeing from reality— and thus as resistance. Yet as it turned out, fairy-tale performances were sought especially after stressful role-playing sessions. This connection became particularly clear if the patients, by having to introduce or role-play important persons in their lives, had had their feelings of loyalty hurt. Whenever the team of therapists was also of the opinion that a less stressful situation was called for, the desire for a fairy-tale performance was permitted. Soon it became apparent that the problems of the various patients in the ward corresponded to their choice in fairy tales and the (conscious and unconscious) modifications thereof. Often it proved easier to work through the patients' basic problems and conflicts on the supernatural fairy-tale level than on an exclusively realistic level.

- *Highly structured fairy-tale performances*

Originally, the entire therapist team and the concerned group of patients would gather fitting fairy-tale themes in the days preceding a performance. Thus, sibling-like problems existing among a number of patients often led them to choose *The Wolf and the Seven Kids, Snow-White* (on account of the seven dwarfs) or, if elements of pseudo-motivation and fear of confrontation were present, *The Seven Swabians*. If conflicts among two or three "siblings" were present, stories such as *The Table, the Ass and the Stick, Cinderella,* but also *Little Brother and Sister* and *Hansel and Gretel* and many others were considered. *The Shoes that Were Danced to Pieces* fit not only instances of having secrets from one's parents, but as well when working through jealousies or rivalries, for example, when several "princesses" desired a single "prince" or vice versa. Incipient friendship and trust could also be implemented if the dance couples remained constant. We did, however, prefer tales such as *Jorinde and Joringel* or *Rapunzel,* etc., for the phases of meeting, for separation and return. The position of man and woman in partnerships can be dealt with very naturally via several fairy tales: the parents in *Hansel and Gretel* and in *The Fisherman and His Wife,* the princess' path of learning and suffering in *King Thrushbeard.*

For us the following condition was important: Any single fairy tale should offer many different ways of confronting the situations and problems reigning in the ward—and at the same time touch on the deep-seated problems of as many of the individual patients as possible. As well, inhibitions and attitudes were to be considered [10]. We discussed in advance whether the one or the other patient should be offered a leading role in a performance, or whether it would be better to give the person a small, marginal role through which he or she could introduce own difficulties and possibilities. In their evening preparations, the patients themselves—in the absence of the therapists—made very humorous and amusing suggestions that were often better than those of the team. (Their tendency, by the way, to tease each other with the roles of a particular tale may have had some influence here.)

At the beginning of the group work, the suggestions were written on the blackboard, and one was chosen to be performed. Each participant, whether patient or clinic personnel, had one vote. Thus, when, say, 15 patients were there, the five or six clinic therapists and nurses as well as the creative therapist present had a good chance of getting their choice elected. Sometimes a certain fairy tale was suggested to the patients with explicit reasoning. Then the original text was read aloud by a single patient, usually chosen by the others (see p. 18), and the creative therapist listed the roles on the blackboard.

For example: *The Wolf and the Seven Kids.* The characters were:

- the old nanny goat
- six kids
- the youngest kid
- the wolf
- the grocer
- the baker
- the miller
- (house door)
- (grandfather clock)
- (well)

(Members of the team in this clinic could not be chosen to assume roles, by the way. I should note at this juncture that, in my opinion, many difficulties in so-called therapeutic communities could be avoided or at least mitigated if patients were fully aware of what can be dealt with democratically and what not. Giving the appearance of greater freedoms than are in reality possible is not wise.)

First, the roles in the performance were distributed, whereby patients were also free to volunteer. Who played what role was then decided by majority vote, each person having one vote per role. For example, when Mrs. X, Miss Y, and Mr. Z were suggested for the role of the old nanny goat, participants had to decide *in advance* whom they wanted. The result, with 15 patients and 6 team members, might have been as follows: Mrs. X—10 votes; Miss Y—4 votes; Mr. Z—7 votes. Thus, Mrs. X played the old nanny goat in the first performance, Mr. Z in perhaps a second one. The therapists were free to cast their votes for a single patient in order to give him or her a fitting role. Only seldom, however, did the therapists make "therapeutic suggestions" for role distribution. For the most part, a suffi-cient majority indeed voted for a suggested role casting if it was fitting or appro-priate.

Next the roles of the youngest kid and the wolf were cast, and only then were the other supporting roles filled: Experience had shown that some participants would volunteer for the minor roles to avoid playing the major ones.

Sometimes it can be advantageous to have people play the role of important objects. Once, in the tale of *The Wolf and the Seven Kids,* a woman depicted a house door that both the wolf and the kids could open only with great force. Working through her own tendencies to both protect and prevent then became a major part of the therapy of this very warm-hearted and considerate woman. To shorten the process, the minor roles are usually not voted on, but rather dis-tributed to other participants not active at the moment, for example, the court la-dies and gentlemen in the tale of the *Frog Prince* or the wild animals in *Show-White.* In the example at hand, the six kids were chosen without further differ-entiation, the first six suggestions sufficing. When role distribution had been completed, the stage area was cleared and the (few) rules explained: Observe any deviations, small or large, from the original; observe the way the role is played; and observe the body language used. Important were also any differences appear-ing between the first and the second performance. All observations were to be brought up in the subsequent discussion.

Neither the therapists nor the audience nor the participants were to give any directions—no whispering and no prompting were allowed, though certain types of help were foreseen. Thus, a character could not say, for example, to Hansel: "Now you've got to drop the pebbles!" or correct something he had done, for ex-ample, if he had used pebbles or pieces of glass instead of crumbs on the second trip through the forest. Gretel could say, however: "Oh, Hansel, don't you have anything that might help us to find our way home?" or (if Hansel had wrongly wanted to drop the pieces of glass): "There are so many clouds today, I don't think the moon will shine tonight—you couldn't even see diamonds in such darkness!" (See also p. 102, the door scene of the *Frog Prince*.)

For those leading the group it was not always easy to simply let matters develop unchecked, for example, when long or tedious scenes occurred or when the entire play was turned into a farce. Yet such tendencies all have their group-dynamic and personal roots—and for the therapeutic situation it was more important to discover these than to put on a perfect fairy-tale performance. Furthermore, if time allowed, the pendulum would usually swing back of its own accord in the other direction when the same fairy tale was performed a second time. The second cast had already been chosen at the beginning, though occasionally the patients sought changes in the casting of one role or the other after the experiences with the first group. This, too, was done by voting; sometimes a person designatedfor a particular role in the second performance wanted to use the opportunity to "resign" from a role. Relatively seldom, however, did the new suggestion derive from personal attitudes toward the person already chosen for a particular role.

In order to guarantee an unbiased second performance, the discussion of the first was delayed, spontaneous comments even being forestalled for later. Rarely was the acting of a character in the first performance so fascinating that it was repeated in the second; rather, the need and desire of the "understudy" to form the character anew usually dominated. Another reason why the two performances were often very different appeared to lie in the choice of fairy tale: If the first performance showed strong tendencies to modify or redo the tale, that called for the second to adhere to the more traditional form. Especially farcical interpretations were often followed up by performances that were replete with deeply felt, serious, and symbolic sentiments. Vice versa, "true and faithful" interpretations led to complete changes in the themes and course of the second performance. This dialectic was also clearly present in individual performances when the participants strived either to modify the tale or remain true to it. For example, in the above-mentioned performance of *Hansel and Gretel,* Hansel, in contrast to the original text, wants to find his way home, and Gretel stops his plan by introducing the darkness in which pieces of glass cannot be seen.

After the performance or performances, we first elicited the experiences of the participants and the observations of the other patients as audience. The therapeutic team was very reserved in revealing its own impressions, and above all no interpretations or conclusions were to be offered that might negatively influence the patients willingness to respond spontaneously and freely. If differences arose between or among patients, the group leader or creative therapist had to transform the either-or situation into an both-and one: Not only were all vantage points viewed as being possible, they were emphasized as being very important in their respective relevance. Then the discussion could, depending on the interests and goals present,

turn to the various behaviors and experiences of the participants, emphasize group-dynamics, or study the various levels present in the fairy tale itself.

Examples:

The Wolf and the Seven Kids: See page 68 for part of the role-selection process. Here, I emphasize only scenes in which the subsequent discussion was important—for *this* group only, of course. We begin with the wolf knocking on the door for the first time. The youngest kid makes a bolt and hides behind one of the "big sisters," played by Ms. A.

Ms. B (to the youngest kid): Oh, don't be such a scaredy-cat!

Ms. A (to Ms. B, while holding the youngest kid in her arms): Don't act as though you've never been afraid.

Wolf (with scratchy voice): Open up, children, your mother is there and has brought something along for each of my dears.

Mr. C: Oh good, Mother is there already . . . (runs to the door)

Mr. D (stopping Mr. C): Are you crazy, can't you hear that it's not the voice of our mother?

Ms. E (softly): What should we do?

Ms. F (with an inquisitive look toward the door): Whether that's really the wolf?

Ms. A: Some day you'll be eaten alive . . . (to Ms. B) Do something!

Ms. B (to the door): You're not our mother, she has a more delicate voice . . .

Wolf: No, no, I am . . . I'm just a little hoarse.

Mr. D: You must think we're dumb . . . you *are* the wolf, for sure.

While the wolf is getting some chalk from the grocer, the scene with the kids continues. Ms. A is now helping the youngest kid—"just to be sure"—to find a good hiding place; Ms. B and Mr. D argue about who of them is the leader and who the smartest. Mr. C is calling for the mother, Ms. E has retreated to a corner, while Ms. F is standing watch at the window.

Wolf (in falsetto): . . . and has brought something along for each of my dears. (laying a hand with dark mitten on the door)

Mr. C (already on the way to the door, nearly ecstatic): Now it's Mother, I recognize her voice!

Mr. D (stopping him): That would not be a very wise thing to do.

Ms. B: Don't you see the black paw?

Ms. F: Oh, oh, how exciting!

Ms. A (holding the youngest kid in her arms): Now don't be afraid, we won't let him in.

Ms. E (is still in her corner, murmuring to herself)

Ms. B (loud): Look at the paw . . .

Mr. D (cutting her off): . . . You're the wolf!

The wolf now goes off to fetch batter and flour. The miller can only just be restrained from killing the wolf by a female patient, who jumps in to play his wife.

In the meantime, Mr. C has developed an even more intensive desire for his "mama." Mr. D and Ms. B are arguing whether the eldest or the most intelligent of them should be in control. Ms. A is taking care of both Mr. C and the youngest kid. Ms. E is reading a "book," and Ms. F roams from window to window to see "what's happening."

Wolf: . . . has brought something along for each of my dears.

Mr. C: Now that is Mother, finally!

Ms. B (curt and sharp): Shut up!

Mr. D: First show us your paw.

Wolf (laying a white glove on the door): If you please.

Some in the audience laugh at such conventional behavior.

Mr. C (rejoicing): You see, it is Mother.

Ms. F (disappointed): Yes, it appears so.

Ms. A: First take a good look.

Ms. E (does not look up from her "book")

Mr. C, held back by no one now, runs to the door and shoves back the bolt. The wolf rushes in, Mr. C being crushed behind the door. In the ensuing chaos and cries of "The wolf, the wolf!" Ms. A remains cool and shoves the youngest kid into the clock case. The others hide as best as possible. Ms. E ducks down and Ms. F stands behind a table with a look on her face as if to say: "Catch me if you can!" Ms. A has not had any time to find a hiding place and is eaten first by the wolf. Ms. E is the next victim. Ms. F dances around the table standing between herself and the wolf. The wolf doesn't bother with her, but rather finds and devours Mr. D and Ms. B. As he comes near the door where Mr. C is hiding, Mr. C calls out "Mama, Mama!", thus giving himself away, and he too is devoured like the others, the wolf saying to him: "Come here, you little squirt." Then the wolf turns to Ms. F and says: "So you want to play with me, huh?" After Ms. F has succeeded in evading him and fleeing for a few minutes, the wolf, now out of breath, wheezes: "This makes me all the more hungry" and eats Ms. F, as well. Then the wolf makes a few rounds in the room and says: "Wasn't there another treat here somewhere? . . . (he sniffs) . . . it smells here of young kid . . . oh, but I am so tired and full . . . I think I'll just lie down in the shade for a while."

After the rescue by the nanny goat, who expresses great joy at finding her kids again, Ms. B and Mr. D accuse each other of being unable to be a leader. Mr. C and the youngest kid are, quite literally, hanging onto their mother. Ms. A reports to the old nanny goat that she had succeeded in hiding the youngest goat. Ms. E goes back to her corner, and Ms. F complains about the "dumb wolf" who devoured her so quickly.

Here, I do not want to discuss the possible meanings of this fairy tale—the development phases, the necessity of being "devoured," the confrontation with one's own greed (on the subject level), the ability to "devour," the use of threats and one's cleverness. Rather, I would like to concentrate on two matters: first, the connections between the personality structure of the respective "kids" and their attitudes during the performance; and second, a description of the discussion of the participants concerning the sibling situation.

- The woman who played the youngest kid stood in real life under the wings of some of the older patients, and all—including the woman herself—thought it quite natural that she had received the most votes to play this role. Being small and in need of protection corresponded for the most part to her life history. Her attempts to free herself of these dependencies had caused phobic symptoms, arrhythmia, and feelings of weakness and faintness.

- Ms. A was helper and victim par excellence. If she felt rejected, she reacted with depressions and cold symptoms.

- Ms. B had set very high standards for herself, and suffered from stress and tension headache that "sometimes developed into migraine attacks."

- Mr. C was a manager with hyperdynamic circulatory disorders; he was always very responsible, kind, and thoughtful. He had received an anti-role: He would have rather played the wolf and out of spite chose the role of a "small little kid." He was amazed, he said, at how much fun it had been.

- Mr. D suffered from severe uncertainty and sweated profusely when he wanted to or had to get things done. For him, as one of the older patients, it was important to be taken seriously—not to "go under."

- Ms. E was in real life also very quiet, standing mostly off-stage; but she was liked by some of her co-patients for her earnestness, tolerance, and her interest in cultural matters. She was in a life crisis: Her own ideals and ideologies were blocking her contact with the others in the group.

- Ms. F had varied, changing symptoms, for the most part minor somatic disorders; she had wanted to be a more interesting animal than a kid. She was unable to come to grips with her own inner life because of continually new, at first very inviting possibilities and persons.

The sibling situation of the seven kids played a major role in the subsequent working-through phase, not the least because there was a large measure of rivalry and competition among the patients on the ward at the time. On the other hand, such behavior also mirrored the old conflicts present in the original families of the patients—a transference phenomenon. Under these circumstances the therapeutic team tried to judge how much both tension within the team and the leadership strategy adopted in the hospital contributed to the intensity of these themes.

Here, a section from the discussion phase:

Observer (Ob) 1 (female): I would have thought that you kids would have held together more.

Observer 2 (male): Yeah, you know, the sheep gather together when the wolf comes . . .

Ob 1: You were more like in a normal human family.

Ms. E: Well, not everyone is like a goat. (This was an attack on the—in her opinion—improper behavior of Ms. F and Mr. C, but also the "stupid rivalry" between Ms. B and Mr. D, even the "blind love" of Ms. A.)

Ms. F (reacting promptly and sharply): You and your noble seclusion—do you know what that leads to: loneliness!

Ms. E: Well, that's better any day than the muddle you're always in.

Ms. A: Now, don't fight, ladies . . .

Mr. C (no longer in the role of the smallest kid, but once again the manager): Yes, please, let us make something constructive of this . . . So, who would like to begin?

Mr. D: Well, I, being the oldest, could . . .

Ms. B (interrupting him immediately): What is that supposed to mean "I being the oldest"? Ms. A was the oldest kid!

Ms. A: I thought that you two (pointing to Ms. B and Mr. D) were the oldest of the kids?

Mr. D (to Ms. B): There, you see, and I was the older brother!

Ms. B (somewhat sarcastic): Maybe, maybe . . . but not the oldest of the brothers and sisters—our proud Ms. E was certainly that.

Ms. E (calmly): I am not proud! I don't even know whether I fit into the bunch of kids.

Ms. F (with a chuckle): Maybe you're an illegitimate child of our Mother.

Creative Therapist: We could all—everyone on his or her own—make a list of the brothers and sisters and then discuss further.

Mr. C: Oh, yes, and we should write the age down beside each.

All were agreed, sheets of paper were distributed, all noted their guesses, and the results were written on the blackboard. The greatest surprise for most was that the kids among themselves judged each other to be much older than one would have expected on te basis of the written text. Those in the audience as well had made high estimates.

It is also interesting that many felt Ms. B and Mr. D to be rival siblings of approximately the same age; only Mr. D judged himself to be older. The only figure judged uniformly was Mr. C, as the second youngest (he had made himself "small" in all respects). Ms. F saw herself as the fifth kid, six years old, something the others could hardly believe: They had judged her to be in her teens. When she protested and pleaded her innocence, the others first laughed, then someone from the audience said: "Maybe the wolf is like your father whom you had wrapped around your finger by the age of six." At this junction, the participants—at the suggestion of the therapist—began comparing the different guesses with their own position in the group of kids. For example: Ms. E was thought by some to have been an only child, quiet and protected. "Oh, by no means," she answered, "I am the third of five children, I have two sisters and two brothers. At home, though, it was always so loud, I liked it better at my grandma's, who had a lot of books and taught me to distinguish flowers and went to concerts with me."

In the subsequent discussion of the different interpretations possible for this fairy tale, the following was distilled:

Obvious morals:

- A mother should never leave her children alone.
- Children should never let a stranger in.
- One learns only by experiencing danger personally.
- The smallest has it best.
- He who eats too much becomes fat and lazy and dies young.

Metamorphic meanings

- The old nanny goat represents well-intentioned, but unfounded admonitions.
- The nanny goat's departure makes developmental progress possible.
- The wolf represents confrontation with greed, with cleverness, and with unchecked fulfillment of desire.
- The wolf could be the father.
- The kids in the present performance correspond to the various ages and developmental stages of a young human being.
- The youngest kid is—unintentionally—the hero of the story.

- If we take the fairy tale to represent the situation of a human being, then it shows how greed can win the upper hand if maturity is not "at home," and how hard it can be to deal with that.

Ms. F noted that she felt it sad that the wolf had to die in the end. Another patient comforted her with the words: "Well, there'll be other interesting animals." Finally, the group discussed whether the fairy tale *The Wolf and the Seven Kids* was a maturation tale or rather an allegorical fable: Both possibilities were held to be equally acceptable.

Transitions

A few patients, particularly those who had already taken part in fairy-tale performances, felt that the transition from the real-life situation to the supernatural world was missing in this tale. The group finally agreed that the entire story took place in fairy-tale land, the kids being able to speak from the beginning. A previous fairy-tale performance had been of *Frau Holle*. There, the therapist, while explaining the matter of the "internal and external mother," had made a sketch of the path taken by Goldmarie and Pechmarie, shown in the figure in a slightly modified form.

In this fairy tale the transitions between the real world and the fairy-tale world are very clear. Entry is gained through the well, which even shows the change in consciousness: "She blacked out, and when she awoke and regained consciousness, she was . . ." The transition on the way back is the archway, and for the others the return is announced by the rooster.

REAL WORLD

FAIRY-TALE WORLD = INNER WORLD

Transitions and metamorphoses usually invoke very strong emotional involvement, be it despair, sadness, fear, devotion, joy, or whatever. If, during a fairy-tale performance, tendencies to change the tale or trivialize it arise, they mostly occur at such junctions. Once in a performance of *Cinderella,* for example, no sorrow was shown by Cinderella at the death of the mother, no tear was shed at her grave, the tree was not watered, the helpful birds were not thanked (see also p. 60). The Prince played his role well, but the birds pecked out Cinderella's eyes instead of those of her "evil" stepsisters. The group then had the desire to experience a "real" Cinderella, so that the second performance was particularly true to the fairy tale. The difference between playing a role and being in the role became evident and no longer had to be expressly showed.

- *Less structured fairy-tale performances*

As mentioned earlier, it is sometimes not only possible but also advantageous to proceed in a less structured manner, assuming the ego strength of the participants, group cohesion, the therapist's own experience, and the continuity of group work allow it. As an example I have chosen parts of the second performance of *Rumpelstiltskin* (see also p. 31).

The workshop was part of a course in psychodrama offered by a Moreno Institute. Before *Rumpelstiltskin,* two other fairy tales had already been performed, the first of which had begun with a democratic distribution of roles in the manner described by Clauser [4]. With the second tale, a "personal" fairy tale (see p. 9), the author had explicitly requested choosing the players herself. So it came that in the second performance of *Rumpelstiltskin* the group wanted to choose the—in their opinion—best players in an unstructured manner. The performance was very true to the original, Rumpelstiltskin being depicted excellently by an older woman, who in turn inspired the others players as well. Besides much praise, both for the entire group and especially for Rumpelstiltskin, the only psychological information on neurosis emerging in the following sharing and feedback phase [36, 39] was the statement of a participant: "It was great, but I always thought Rumpelstiltskin was a male figure." The woman who had played the role was of the opinion that that was of no consequence for the fairy tale. And besides, her Rumpelstiltskin was not a woman but a supernatural power—a power that was no longer needed when the miller's daughter had gained enough experience on her own and had become superior.

The woman who had played the miller's daughter confirmed that before voicing Rumpelstiltskin's name a great feeling of power had overcome her. The others agreed: They had noticed how, during the performance, she had said the words slowly and with visible pleasure: "Is . . . your . . . name . . . perhaps . . . . . . Rumpelstiltskin?!" Particularly the pause before the name itself had raised the tension considerably. Some participants mentioned then, however, that in the written fairy tale Rumpelstiltskin is indeed called a manikin. It was agreed to play the tale once more. Now, besides having a man play Rumpelstiltskin, the group felt it important to choose people who could play the typical boastful father, a real king, etc.

The performance began with the miller, overzealous about his daughter, singing her praises to a group of friends, one of whom told the story of the daughter's special talents to the king. The king was somewhat pathetic in his "God-given duties." At his disposal was a private secretary, a steward, a company of bodyguards—and a complete royal household in which all others who had no role had to serve. The miller was "ordered" to appear before the court, to repeat his tale, only then to be sent off with a majestic gesture—the miller, in fact, disappeared completely after that. The miller's daughter was then, at the order of the king, brought to the castle by a bodyguard and taken to a chamber full of straw, where the king tersely confronted her with her new duty. One of the king's guards stood watch before the door. The miller's daughter cried her eyes out, and then appeared a very lively Rumpelstiltskin, who apparently liked the miller's daughter very much. He said, in a very friendly manner: "What will you give me if I spin the straw for you?" "My necklace," the miller's daughter answered and gave it to him. The manikin then went about his work with a mixture of self-assuredness, primitiveness, and complete adoration for the beautiful maid. The next morning, upon seeing the gold, the king became obsessed and wanted more. He ordered all court helpers to roam the countryside and bring back straw, enough to fill a giant chamber: The miller's daughter had become his means to riches. Some of the bodyguards were already murmuring against him.

In the second night the captain of the guard stood watch personally. Rumpelstiltskin appeared at the maid's first lamentations and offered to "fix everything for her." He forgot to request something of her, but was reminded of this by the miller's daughter, who asked him what he wanted this time. Rumpelstiltskin put both hands on her shoulders, looked long and tenderly into her eyes and said: "Well . . . what? (sigh) . . . Okay, give me your ring." The miller's daughter took off her ring and placed it on the manikin's little finger, who viewed the ring joyfully and stroked the girl's hair. Then he began spinning gold.

On the following day, the king was even more majestically inclined: He now saw nothing but the gold and even forgot his promise to take the miller's daughter for his wife if she were to spin gold out of the straw he had had stacked in the largest room in the castle. The king's steward reminded him of this, whereupon the king said: "Yes, of course . . . of course you shall become my wife. (aside:) Then I shall have gold in abundance." The king himself sat at the main entrance to the castle that night, and guards were placed at all doors. The miller's daughter, in a voice with no trace of doubt, said: "I'm sure the manikin will come again . . ." And Rumpelstiltskin suddenly appeared; but before he could request "a living being," the miller's daughter (MD) pointed out to him the great amount of straw in the room: "The greedy king wants so much gold." To which Rumpelstiltskin (R) replied: "And will you marry him?"

MD: Oh, he only sees the gold. And I don't like him at all. But what can I do . . . he has the all the power.

R (looking directly at her): I have an idea, but I don't know whether you'll like it.

MD (eager): Oh, what is it? . . . Please tell me!

R: You could go with me into the woods, to my little house in the forest where no one could find us. We could just forget the king . . . and (with a questioning look to the girl) stay together.

MD: Oh, yes, let's do that! . . . But what if the king follows us?

R: He won't find us . . . Let him suffocate in his gold . . . I'll spin it for him (sits down and begins spinning) buzz, whirr, whizz, purr . . . So, it's finished!

With a magical gesture Rumpelstiltskin opens the doors. The king awakes, sees them running off, and sends his guards after them. The captain of the guard is fastest and catches up with the miller's daughter.

MD: Oh, please, Sir, let me go with Rumpelstiltskin. I simply can't stay with the king and marry him.

Some of the guards now arrive, one of whom says: "I'm tired of serving him, too. Nothing but carrying out his orders, and not a word of praise. Threats and punishment, that's all it is." The other guards agreed.

R: Here in the woods there's lots of room, you could be your own boss and build your own house.

MD: Oh, yes . . . let the devil take the king.

Captain: Without soldiers I, too, shall not serve the king . . . I'll go with you.

King (calling out loud): Come back . . . come back—immediately! I order you to come back. Otherwise, I'll have you caught and punished.

Guard (calling back): Well, who's going to do that work for you now?

Everyone laughs, and they all go into the forest.

Even before everyone in the group had taken a seat, the man who played the king complained that the others had digressed too much from the fairy tale and left him alone: He, after all, had done only what was required of him. To which the others replied: "Are you kidding me?" "Such an egotistical despot!" "Who wants to be a pawn for such a king?" The man playing the miller said: "You know, I didn't even exist for you, neither as a human being nor as a father." The king defended himself by referring to the original text of the fairy tale (for the most part, by the way, correctly) in which the king is only interested in the gold; he was not able to marry the miller's daughter only because the others had changed the story completely around. The woman playing the miller's daughter answered: "That's not true! You forgot your promise to make me your wife." But the king persisted: "You said you wanted a *real king* . . . and I tried to play that role." The group leader confirmed this, which calmed the man enough to allow another comment: "But I do believe that the majestic and egotistical behavior of the king lead to the others' desire to change the text. On the other hand, I don't believe that the king's behavior alone was the cause for the changes. Let's look at the different tendencies and motives that played a role."

The man playing the captain said he would have liked to have had the miller's daughter for his own, but that he hadn't dared to revolt against the king. And he was scared of being rejected by her. He then brought this thought into connection with his own real-life situation: He had once suppressed his own plans for a career change, much as he had once not dared to express his deep feelings for someone, both of which he regretted even today.

A woman in the audience noted that Rumpelstiltskin's request "Give me, when you have become queen, your first-born child" was missing from the performance, something she regretted: She had always like the place most where Rumpelstiltskin says "No, a living being is more dear to me than all the treasures of this world." The man playing Rumpelstiltskin answered by laying his arm around the miller's daughter and saying: "Don't worry, I did get a living being." "Yeah, sure," the woman said, "but not a child." "I don't see where the problem lies? (grins) The child will surely come along, don't you think?"

Many of the group members were not unhappy that the text had been changed, but were rather dissatisfied with the "simple solution" of Rumpelstiltskin's becoming the new partner of the miller's daughter. Here, the therapist made the suggestion that each member change the story from a certain place onward of his or her own choice (see p. 31).

Other examples on performing folk and maturation tales or scenes may be found on pages 68 and 103. With fairy-tale-like literary stories (see p. 8) and with fairy tales of other cultures, it is important that not only the client who suggests the performance be interested in the themes represented there, but that the themes and problems discussed be relevant to the entire group. On the other hand, in a group that is already working together well, the suggestion of performing an unknown tale may indeed be acceptable and may in fact touch depths otherwise unreachable.

Tales from Other Cultures

Here, I shall mention only one example (see page 7). When performing tales from other cultures, it can be advantageous to adapt the work method not only in accordance with the many factors mentioned above—patient or group member, role of therapist, type of therapy, therapy goal—but as well to the character of the fairy tale at hand.

In a seminar on the psychodrama of fairy tales, after a number of well-known maturation tales had been performed, a participant introduced a tale that had apparently fascinated him: *The Three Winds and the Volcano,* which to my knowledge stems from Indonesia. The story was difficult to understand when read aloud. Only after the man had told it in his own way did the group "catch fire." Yet some doubts emerged whether the tale could be performed at all, one participant saying that he couldn't imagine what one would say or do in the role of the wind, the people, a volcano, or Nico (who survives the volcano to carry on traditions). Thus, the group decided to give a pantomimic presentation, with music and sound effects. A fixed form was selected, in part to help the players to follow the temporal order of the story's events.

There were the following roles and events:

- the winds and their meeting

- the peoples in the time before the volcano eruption

- the volcano eruption

- the time after the eruption

- Nico and the rebuilding of the village.

What actually happened during the performance cannot be completely caught in words. The following is my attempt at a description.

The winds, each of them of a different character, appeared one after the other. Three to four group members formed each of the winds and were spontaneously set into motion through purely acoustical signals. They ran, strode, glided, and rushed through the room; when the winds met, there occurred something like a mythical dance drama [38].

Then came part two. The story read as follows: "And the years passed like hours, a hundred years like a day." The different "peoples" each had their own signs: In one case they were shoulder scarfs, in another hats or signs drawn directly on the face. Differences also rapidly appeared in the way they moved, supported by differences in the noises they made, in their rhythms and "music." After the first tentative meetings, a rather noisy, chaotic bustle occurred, much like at a fair. The relatively hard staccato of the one group mingled with the sing-song of a second—and this with the grumblings of a third. Suddenly, in the middle of all this, someone became "time": He pounded on the seat of a turned-over wooden chair, first at rather long intervals of 8–10 seconds, in between making half-moon motions with his hand in the air, the palm of which he directed toward the group. Everyone understood that this depicted the sun's journey of one day's time. Then the pounding became faster and faster.

When the interval was down to 2–3 seconds, the depiction of the sun stopped, and the days raced by at four to five per second. This rapid passing of time was truly gripping, something I'm sure is hard to comprehend upon reading these lines in the normal intellectual/rational manner. But perhaps the reader can get some of the feel by shutting the eyes and being transported into the situation—or better, by taking the time to experience for oneself how the days rush by ever more quickly.

The activity of the various peoples then calmed and quieted down: Everyone was listening to the "time," to the years passing. A feeling of transitoriness became apparent, a "knocking" at timelessness' and eternity's door!

At this juncture the first thunderings of the volcano were heard, and the performance slipped into the third scene. Rumbling was heard, hissing, blubbering—an ever-increasing cacophony of noises of all types filled the air and took hold of the audience. Here, one could experience that, as one participant phrased it in the following discussion, "it was only possible to stand such noise if you were making it yourself." The "houses and villages," built of available chairs, benches, tables, and blankets during the meeting of the peoples, were destroyed completely. When the volcano ceased erupting, chaos ruled the room.

Then there were a few minutes of quietude; they were experienced as being very, very long and represented the time after the eruption.

The storyteller eventually began reciting again. He reported the emergence of the old Nico, who had survived the volcano eruption and, after a long journey, had discovered other humans alive.

Life began to return to the scene, at first slowly, as though one hardly dared to move. Then a few participants started wandering around in the mess. They nodded to each other as they passed. Nico leaned on a shepherd's staff and demonstrated with gestures how he had experienced the eruption of the volcano. Some of the participants began building a hearth protected from the wind, others built huts with beds. Later, no one could say for sure who had begun work on the temple; but it was certain that one participant had set up two foam-rubber parts from a sofa of about 1 meter length and another had placed a third over the top to form a portal. Nico then built an altarpiece below it. (Yet none of the four temple-builders held himself for the one who had the *idea* of building a temple in the first place.) In the meantime, the "village" bustled: Couples and families had been formed. Nico walked around the village, using his shepherd's staff as a weapon, and stood guard. But when two participants played sheep, Nico once again gladly became a shepherd, and the others made him their "wise man." The performance ended in an idyllic pastoral scene: the sheep bleating, a high priest reciting a sermon, a good-night song in the air.

Besides those already mentioned above, the themes of time and the transitory nature of things, of destruction and dying, and of resurrection from chaos played the greatest role in the following discussion: *Dying and becoming* was viewed in a perspective spanning centuries. The thought of the newly formed village proved to be comforting, all the more as the eruption of the volcano caused associations to become evident to the modern threat to our lives through atomic dangers and through changes in the ecological balance.

Concerning the technique used in this performance, I should also mention that movement, vibration, and nonverbal acoustic signals can affect us very intensely. Not only are relevant somatic memories freed up, they also appear with a certain vehemence. One should also note that unplanned, spontaneous developments in the plot and time sequences may occur. The man playing "time" reported only that at first he pounded a slow beat—a quiet contrast to the bustle of the others; then he had the idea of the sun's journey; finally it occurred to him to have the years go by ever faster.

Fairy tales, sagas, myths, and songs from foreign cultures have another advantage in their use in psychotherapy: Well-known tales of one's own culture, regardless of how large the interest may be among the participants in seeking out individual experiences, may lead to certain expectations in the *therapist(s)*. After watching the fifteenth or whatever performance of *Sleeping Beauty,* a therapist is bound to be more alert to generally valid aspects than to variations. We view completely unknown or foreign tales, on the other hand, in a less prejudiced manner—we are more open to aspects that, as it were, "don't fit." Thus, in courses for continuing education I always suggest that one employ the one or other foreign tale.

Personal Fairy Tales

Even during the getting-acquainted phase a therapist can begin leading the participants of a seminar or course toward consideration of personal fairy tales, by suggestions such as the following: "Maybe you could all introduce yourselves with the name you'd like to be called during the time here. That could, for example, be a favorite name. Or you could use a figure or a story that especially touched you. Personal fairy tales as well as the more well-known traditional tales are equally welcome."

After a few of the more well-known fairy tales have been performed, the group's interest often turns automatically toward unknown stories, so that it becomes very easy to perform a personal tale or to have the group invent one.

- *In a strict sense*

Here, I would like to mention a few of the most important aspects stemming from the performance of the tale *The Elf Queen* (see p. 12).

The author, a woman, did not want to play the lead role, which had, of course, been offered her by the group; rather, she had been thinking the whole time of another woman, who then accepted gladly. The Prince had a difficult role: The river he had to cross consisted of all the women in the group, who together formed tempting, alluring, pulling, devouring waves that dragged him down such that he could reach the shore only after great effort. And every time he was about to give up, the old woman fired him on (something that was not in the original tale). But it became even worse when he had to fight the dragon, which, so the story went, he was to defeat. The Prince had understood this as meaning to *kill* the dragon, whereas the dragon had interpreted it as a number of tasks he was to pose the Prince who then had to solve them. In any case, the dragon could not be "killed," and over and over he forced the Prince back to the shore of the river—and again in the "arms of the waves." For a moment the Prince forgot his role and said to some of the women (the waves): "Okay, okay, you all are overcome, so stop it now!" Then he whacked the head of the dragon off and said: "So there, now you're dead!" "No, I'm not," the dragon answered, "I have many heads, and any cut off grow back quickly." To which the Prince replied: "Well, for me you're dead." Then he jumped into the field where the Elf Queen sat playing thoughtfully on her flute. The Prince suddenly became quiet, sat still for a long time, listened to her playing, and was completely involved in it, without trying to draw attention to himself or to force matters. After a while he put his hands, palms up, on his knees, which were very close to those of the Elf Queen. Then she looked up and noticed his hands. Slowly she lifted her gaze and looked him straight and calmly in the eyes. Then they took each other's hand and the old woman, who had been so concerned about the Prince, said: "The tasks have now been fulfilled." And to the Elf Queen: "You are free."

In the following discussion the man playing the Prince said that, upon nearing the Elf Queen after all the tortures he had experienced with the river and the dragon, he had the strong feeling that it was not the time for action, for achievements, for conquering. It made him feel uneasy—and it stirred him. The flutist felt understood and accepted, just like the author of the tale. The extremely strong erotic/sexual overtones of the deed of "going-through-the-raging-river-for-someone" surprised the others. And the women who played the waves had not agreed beforehand on being sirens. The misunderstanding between the Prince and the dragon proved to be fruitful for both: Their contradictory positions— killing is the final defeat versus killing is not a defeat—were discussed extensively. The man who played the dragon said: "He wanted to get rid of me quickly, but he didn't want to have to deal with me, to learn from me, or accept anything of mine. If he'd at least wanted to bathe in my blood or eat my heart or do something else to gain my strength, it would have been different. But he was in a hurry to get to the Elf Queen. It's only good that his effectivity didn't help him any there, but that he had to learn to act differently."

The author herself was interested in the subject level. How could the wise old woman, the deeply absorbed flutist, the tempting waves of the river, and the dragon work together such that all parts, especially the male and female elements, be in harmony with each other? The flutist did not see the situation in the same way: To her it depicted the awakening of a woman by a man who cannot only resist temptations and brazen through danger, but who has the rare ability to be present without necessarily resorting to action. Without this presence on the same "wavelength," the Elf Queen would never have turned her gaze to him—or even had the desire to do so.

- *Texts written by the group*

Here, we may be dealing with the tale of some particular member of the group (see the above as well as the "utility tale" given below), of several members and the group (pp. 36), or of the entire group (pp. 43).

An example:

At the beginning of the fifth, and last, 3-hour group session, a participant gave an improvised puppet show on a "stage" constructed of two chairs with a piece of cloth spanned between their upright backs. Only the two puppets could be seen, the puppeteer being hidden and appearing only when the "gamemaster" was required. The following is a free translation of the original.

The Odd Couple, starring Mr. Id (ID) and Ms. Superego (SE) (and the showmaster, SM)

SM: Listen folks, now listen to me,
for I've story to tell all of thee
about Mr. Id and Ms. Superego—
whether you'll like it, I really don't know.
If you don't, well it's no shame,
but do keep quiet, just the same.
ID (with a growl): A good old Neanderthal am I,
I'm happy as can be and I don't know why.
SE: Well, well, such a frolicking song at this hour!
ID: Madam, I'm not always a puss that's sour . . .
SE: Shhhh, your language's too rich.
ID: Not like that of some other bitch
I know.
SE: Oh, these harsh words!
ID: Madam, they are my swords.
They come and they go,

I've got no control,
suddenly it itches,
then it twitches,
up and down, from bottom to top.
SE: Well, it certainly's got to stop.
Words straight out of Babel
you don't find them in Scrabble.
You'll have to take more care
and watch out for my share
or I shall not be well . . .
ID: You can send such talk to hell!
SE: Oh, God, I feel I must faint,
of course, I knew you were no saint.
But now I see, where I can sit
that the two of us just don't fit.
ID: Now, now, stop that drivel,
I don't get it, where's the trouble?
SE: The trouble? I dare say!
How'd you like it, the live long day
without me, alone, wouldn't you miss . . .
ID: Oh, leave me alone, I've got to piss. (leaves)
Ahhhh, a relief for that bladder of mine,
comes from drinking that Neanderthal wine. (reappears)
Can I get that here, that wonderful juice
that gives me strength and force profuse?
SE: Well, I can do without such rant.
ID: I'm sure you can, but I sure can't.
And speaking of aunt and nieces, my dear . . .
SE: Oh, now he's getting obscene, I fear,
I spoke not a word of aunts or nieces!
ID: You really bore me to pieces!
Why, if you're so frigid yourself,
won't you let me partake of the wealth
of nieces in the world?
SE: He's drunk, he's been wine-bibbing.
ID: Or how 'bout partner-swapping?
Oh, doesn't that sound profane?

SE: Let's go, it's about to rain.
ID: Oh, you just want to keep me waiting.
Now, what was it I was contemplating?
Ah yes, my starving self I need to feed.
SE: Oh, how embarrassing, how perfide!
ID: Perfide you say, embarrassing?
I can show you more of such things:
Abrakadabra, here's my wish,
a table, chairs, a great big dish
full to the brim of bread, meat and cheese
and beer to drink, as much as I please.
SE: Oh, people listen, I've must tell ye
this one thinks only of his own belly.
It's so horrible, so perverse,
to hear such awful things—in verse!
ID: And I, I find it awful when . . .
SE: Oh, I suffer such insolence!
ID: I ask you, folks, does she make sense?
That's just my luck, with this "lady" here,
to be stuck, year in, year out,
her wretched moods, her constant pout.
Is there one among you who
sees it fit to walk in my shoe?
SE: What . . . what do you say,
you naughty boy, you debauchee,
I can't stand this one more day.
For what you say makes me ill,
so let us part while we can still
agree at least on that.
ID: So now the torture is all over?
I'm free again, a single lover?
SE: I am free—you are free,
I am determined, so let it be.
ID: Yahoo! Not a day longer with that old bat,
it's great—I could kiss you for that. (he does)
SE: Stop it now, shame on you. Well, good-bye,
and if we ne'r meet till we die . . .

ID: Let's hope not. So I say so long,
I've got much to do, I must be gone.
SE: So let him go—ah, so peaceful here
with Mr. Id no longer near.
ID: Where to go to first, to the East or West,
to find myself a prettier nest?
Or maybe better to the North or South,
to rape and whore and murder about?
To belch and fart and steal and lie,
do all the things make me lady cry.
So farewell, ciao, good-bye.
SE: Au revoir, adieu, ade,
I shan't miss you anyway.

(They go to their respective sides, and only then do they notice that they are bound together by a rope.)

SE: Hey, what is that? What can it be?
ID: It looks as though we can't be free.
SE: I'm stupefied, amazed, irate,
in ways that I cannot relate!
ID: And now that old bag continually
will blow her moral horn at me—
that ugly witch, dumb old bitch . . .
SE: I see I have still much to teach
of manners and respect and shame,
that you shall not blaspheme my name.
Oh, horror, is there no solution?
No way to end this awful pollution?
ID: Please tell us, is there none?
SM: Oh yes, you two, there is one:
Stand back to back and you shall find:
It's out of sight, out of mind.
And now together into the chains! (ties them up)
Like naive folks that note the pains
of the briars they've landed upon
only when there's no more to be done.
ID: But back to back?
SE: Is that the right track?

(they turn in circles, but cannot see each other)

ID: Oh come on now and cut me loose
and don't be such a silly goose!

SE: Ah, thank God, I've now my peace,
and can't I see him, so he shall cease
to exist at all for me, this Id.

ID: If she will not do what I have bid,
so be it: my own life I shall live.
It serves her right that I'll not grieve
to know no more than I perceive.
And what I don't know I surely won't miss,
for the truth is: ignorance is bliss.

SM: And so they live very contentedly
what I would call somewhat differently
than psychologists who say "they repress":
They're seeing these days of each other less.
The point has come to end my cause,
please give the two a great big applause.

The banter going on between Id and Superego should be thought of as an inner dialog, leading to knowledge of their "inseparableness." As well, the pseudo-solution, not unusual in such situations, is depicted as just that. The extremely sensitive author allowed himself a "trip into forbidden realms." The development of the "Neanderthal" surprised some of the other participants who could see this raw-natured figure only as a counterpoint to the "fine lady"—and to the author himself.

The use of self-made puppets has several advantages:

- One's own character traits emerge, be they suppressed or only underdeveloped.

- Characteristic traits of present or past important persons emerge in parodistic form and thus become clear both to the therapist and the creator.

- "Dialogs" may occur while forming and creating, and sometimes the puppet even "demands" a different character than that intended by the creator.

- The attributes of supernatural and fairy-tale figures as designated by the creator are often to be found in their make-up and their behavior.

- It is often easy to make the transition from drawing, painting, and modeling to actual performances via puppets, and from role-playing one can make the transition via "auxiliary egos" to other creative therapy forms.

A final note: Puppet shows such as this not only allow three different roles to be played simultaneously and inner processes to be worked through dramatically, they also offer the possibility of creating transitional or intermediate objects—a temporary invalidity of projections.

I would now like to turn to the performance of *Philipp and Eberhard* (p. 37). To gain a better understanding of the authors and in particular one female participant described in more detail, I would like to follow their way through the free improvisation of the tale (see p. 103).

Recall that after the authors had read the tale aloud, a discussion could not be held, so that the roles were distributed first thing the next day. Some caused no problems: One participant who had already acted in improvisations of *The Brave Little Tailor* and *The Ant Prince* and been the king in another fairy-tale performance, was chosen as chancellor as well as the black knight. Philipp was played by a woman (there were simply too few men), who had played a monk in an anti-role-play. Eberhard was played by an ebullient, agile man, and Herrmann was played by the man who had not wanted to play the priest in the improvisation (see p. 104; the latter was most certainly an anti-role). There were difficulties in picking someone to play Rosalind; suggestions were slow to be made, no one really being interested. Finally someone said: "I'll play Rosalind if I can also play the role of the beautiful girl robbed by the knight." (The same woman, Ms. T, had, by the way, already played the witch in a performance of *Hansel and Gretel* (p. 104) and the dragon who guarded the "treasure" of the women (p. 105) as well as the "letter of the mother" in a performance of *Little Hans*.) The other participants gave a sigh of relief and agreed. It was first suggested that the king be played by the man who later played Herrmann, but in the course of the discussion I myself was pressured to assume this role; of course, I was assured, this should not be interpreted as a "hint" or a "message" of any kind. After a short reassuring look to my co-therapist, who did not play in the piece, I agreed and added with a laugh that at least the part about liking to eat well fit me. The Queen of Aquitania was played by a women who had also taken part in the improvisation of *Little Hans*. The queen's role was assumed by a woman who had desired to play an object in the performance of *Little Hans*.

The plot was discussed under the supervision of the two authors. They suggested reading through each section or act of the play once again before the actual performance. Beyond that they wanted neither to give any instructions nor to direct the performance. One further idea they had took the form of a condition: All the men were to participate in the scene in "The Full Mug," and in the scene in "The Green Wreath," all women. This suggestion was greeted with great laughter.

I would suggest that the reader follow the authors' suggestions and reread the respective sections beforehand.

Act I

A festive table was set up together. In the middle of the one long side sat the queen, to her left the king, there being considerable room between and around them. At the head of the table, to the left of the king, sat the Queen of Aquitania; at the other end sat Philipp; directly across from the king sat Eberhard. The other two chairs were occupied by "make-believe guests."

The king, in an attempt to impress the Queen of Aquitania, spoke of the good qualities of his son Eberhard and generally enjoyed the many wonderful things on the table. The queen was the typical disappointed and jealous wife—as well as an overbearing mother: Philipp considered himself to be at least 14 and at most 16 years of age—but was treated by the mother like a three-year-old. Eberhard wanted to—and indeed was supposed to—be a 20-year-old. He and the Queen of Aquitania showed their mutual interest as it stood in the text, albeit with only little enthusiasm. The angrier the queen became, the more the king occupied himself with the guest. Thus, he somewhat stole the show from Eberhard—despite his grand eulogies of his son—as if to say: "If the father is so great, then you'll just love the son and want to have him for you own." Philipp sat daydreaming; Eberhard demonstrated his defiance by slouching in his chair and later, after the first appearance of the chancellor, directly through childish protest. Only after the chancellor's second warning, when the king told the chancellor to have a seat and join in the festivities, did Eberhard's anger—including his demand to be given a large army—have a true and authentic ring to it. The Queen of Aquitania observed him with great interest and shook her head at the king, who continued to speak of the "boy." The mother looked very contented at the statement that her son should stay at home, and thus reacted very strongly to his plan to leave. She changed the sentence "My son, we love you so much" into "My son, *I* love you so much." When it became clear that Eberhard was serious in his intent to leave and to give up his right to the throne, there was great consternation, which was somewhat placated when the king gave him the three jewels—representing the entire wealth of the kingdom. Neither Philipp nor the chancellor seemed to like that. Philipp's last attempt to hold Eberhard back (supported in this performance by the queen) was rejected with scorn for the "little brother" greater than that mentioned in the text. At the end of Act I, Eberhard has just left the table, the queen is holding "little Philipp" in her arms, the king has once again turned his attention to the meal, the chancellor shakes his head at the whole matter, and the Queen of Aquitania observes Eberhard's exit with great interest.

Act II

The table is then transformed into the inn "The Full Mug." The men in the group gather around the table to drink; one of them plays the innkeeper. Eberhard enters the scene, joined the group, and subsequently a lively and spontaneous scene develops that could rival that at any local pub. A "drinking contest" is then held, which ends with most of the participants under the table, asleep. The innkeeper then wakes Eberhard and demands he pay his bill, whereupon Eberhard gives him one of the three jewels. He waits for a while on his "change," but then leaves without protesting when the innkeeper informs him that he "unfortunately" has no change available.

The scene switches to the inn "The Green Wreath." Now the women in the group, accompanied by the laughter of the men, take their positions. Some exaggerate their roles (out of embarrassment?). One women observes herself in a mirror, others get themselves ready, another woman lies lasciviously on a couch, smoking a cigarette in a long holder. No one is dancing. When Eberhard enters, everyone turns to him, and soon Rosalind goes to him, putting on the charm. They dance a while, she holds him tightly and eventually invites him up to her room. Now the rest of the house is faded out, and the other women return to the audience. Alone, Eberhard and Rosalind show considerable embarrassment and uncertainty; they lie on the bed (two coats spread out), they embrace, but go no further: no caresses, no kisses. From the vantage point of the audience, it looks as though Eberhard would like to hide Rosalind. Then the two of them stand up, and a pause occurs in which no one knows what should really happen next. Rosalind says: "Now you must go," to which Eberhard only reacts with "Oh yes, yes . . . that was short." Now Rosalind returns to her role and replies: "Well, what did you think? Don't you know there are others waiting?" The entire scene is missing the erotic touch present in the text, above all the statement of Rosalind: "You're a noble warrior on the battlefield of desire." Rosalind's request for payment and Eberhard's willful turning over of the second jewel seem artificial and stilted.

The inn scenery is removed. The woman who played Rosalind puts on a white scarf as veil to play the damsel in distress, and the man who played the chancellor has on a black overcoat to play the knight. He drags the helpless girl with him. Eberhard enters and blocks the way. For a second it looks as though Eberhard is prepared to fight the knight, but he has no weapon and thus resorts to negotiating with him. The two are quickly agreed, and Eberhard hands over the rest of his inheritance to the knight. As difficult as it seemed to be for the two participants playing Eberhard and the girl to be comfortable with each other in the last scene, so easy it now appears for them to hold hands. Eberhard bids the girl to come with him, he tells her of his love for her, and they embrace. It is apparently very difficult for the woman to remain true to the role and tell him that she has long been promised to another. And she doesn't simply turn and go, leaving Eberhard standing. Rather she waits until he can part from her of his own free will, though sad and full of reluctance. Eberhard's loneliness, his sadness, and his having wasted the inheritance were present on his face as he turned to travel on, tired and hungry.

The farmer was played by the group leader as a rustic, somewhat gruff old man, though not without a certain warmth. Eberhard is allowed to stay in exchange for tending the pigs. The pigs were played by the members of the audience—and with great enthusiasm, I might add. They grunted, pushed, shoved and wallowed in the mud and generally made it very difficult for Eberhard to tend them. Yet there was also a degree of comfort found in the physical nearness, an attachment, but also rivalry among the pigs for the attention of the keeper. Eberhard hardly had time for the day-dreaming and homesickness required in the text. Eberhard's expression of his longing for the Queen of Aquitania was not in the original text, and nothing was said about his farewell from the farmer. In the performance it is all very harmonious: Eberhard expresses clearly his desire to leave and his thankfulness for having been allowed to stay; the farmer says that he was sorry to lose such a good pig-tender, but that he can understand Eberhard's wish to go.

Act III (in the king's chamber)

The king is lying on his bed; the queen is pacing the floor; Philipp stands in one corner; the chancellor repeatedly enters to bring the bad news of Herrmann's attacks; the "masses" outside the castle can be heard to chant: "Save us, O king!" and "Herrmann is pillaging and ravaging everything!" and "Do something!" Philipp tells his battle plan to defeat Herrmann. His mother not only, as stated in the text, wrings her hands, she clings to him desperately and won't let him go. The woman playing Philipp found it difficult to free herself. Then the queen calls to her husband, but the king hardly reacts, and the queen says: "If Philipp goes, I won't have anyone left." To which the king responds, somewhat meekly: "You'll still have me." "You?" the queen replies sharply and condescendingly.

Change of scenery: Knight's chamber and room of mirrors.

Philipp approaches Herrmann's castle, enters the knight's chamber and, true to the role, calls for peace. Herrmann scorns him, and when Philipp challenges him to a fight and wages his kingdom, Herrmann can hardly control his laughter. After a while, and after repeated calls to draw his sword, Herrmann chases Philipp with a cry "I'll get you." The mirrors are standing at different angles to each other, in part being represented by the backs of chairs. Philipp first stands in front of one of the mirrors and then at the right moment jumps to the side; Herrmann thinks his image in the mirror to be an opponent and breaks the mirror in two with the cry "Now you've had it." He then falls through the opening that appears and into a dungeon below. Herrmann feels disgraced and repeatedly tells Philipp to kill him: He says he simply can't take it being tricked by a boy. Philipp has to plead with Herrmann to accept his mercy, and it almost looked as though Herrmann was the merciful one sparing Philipp the task of killing him. Philipp pulls Herrmann up, gives up his claim to Herrmann's kingdom, and invites Herrmann to a festive peace banquet in the castle of his father.

Act IV (scenery as in Act I)

The queen is sitting between the king (as previously, to her left) and Herrmann (to her right). Philipp and Lisa, Herrmann's daughter, are sitting on the opposite side, close together. The chancellor is seated to the left of the king, where the Queen of

Aquitania had been. Herrmann is trying to woo the queen, who is becoming increasingly interested in his overtures. Lisa and Philipp go out to take a walk. The king observes that Herrmann has laid his hand on the queen's—and that she's begun to lean toward him. The king raises up to a "What are you doing?" to which the queen replies sharply: "Yes, why not me too?" Then she turns her attention back to Herrmann. The festivities have an uneasy atmosphere. Lisa and Philipp return and announce that they have become engaged. Yet before the rejoicing over this can begin, Eberhard enters, clothed in rags, and is recognized. He looks downtrodden and repentant, but he neither cries nor humbles himself. He reports on his experiences at the inn and that he freed the women, and he even mentions his work for the farmer. But he is not willing to tell everyone everything—thus digressing somewhat from his role. The king tries to persuade him to be honest at least to his father, but Eberhard only repeats that he has lost the entire inheritance: He refuses all further information, as he doesn't want to have to tell everything like a "little boy." The king accepts this behavior, chalks up his refusal as a sign of his independence and maturity, and uses it in his reasoning as to why Eberhard should once again have claim to the throne. The scene becomes very much like that of "The Prodigal Son." Before Philipp can become really angry with his father, Lisa comforts him by mentioning that together they are to rule Herrmann's kingdom. The queen, too, tries to soothe Philipp. For a moment it looks as though Philipp has two motherly figures. Lisa then succeeds in making her father rejoice at the thought of becoming a grandfather. In this atmosphere of peace and reunion, Eberhard announces that he must once again go on a journey, but without revealing his destination. His mother is worried, but the king exclaims his understanding and wishes Eberhard luck on his journey. Generally speaking, his announcement is accepted much more easily than the earlier attempts at detachment.

A few passages from the working-through phase will have to suffice. The participants were generally satisfied with the performance. The authors were glad that all had taken part, and that their piece had proved to be quite playable. Mr. R said that he would have liked for Philipp to be treated by the mother more as a teenager, but otherwise he was pleased with the development of the two princes. Eberhard's digression—not wanting to tell all—was accepted, as was Herrmann's statement that he'd rather die than be disgraced. The queen's taking a liking to Herrmann was also considered acceptable, in part as compensation (or punishment) for the king's ways, his egoistic interest in the good life, and his flirting with the Queen of Aquitania. Both the drinking scene at the inn and the scene in which Eberhard tended the pigs were experienced by all as being wonderful and funny. The scene in the bordello provoked a serious discussion about one's own characteristics and needs. How far can one really go and how much freedom can one grant others? In the performance the limits for some at least were moved out only very little. "Acting as though it were so is fine, but actually doing it—no thanks," one female participant said. Rosalind was praised for her courage to have taken the part at all. On the other hand, all were agreed that Eberhard and Rosalind were much too tame in their relations once they were alone. The woman playing Rosalind said that it had been important for her to act out two aspects of being a woman. First, she had been concerned with the problem of death (p. 104); thus, she had wanted to play the witch and die in *Hansel and Gretel*. Second, in the fairy-tale improvisation she had played the dragon whose task it was to guard the women's treasure in the cave (the chapel; cf. Figure VII as well as Figures 6 and 8b, the background; p. 105). There, she had fallen during a fight, had died as a dragon, and been reborn as a woman. Carrying the letter of the mother (p. 108), she had indeed had contact with Little Hans, but only as messenger. Thus, it was important to her to try out different aspects of being a woman. She was pleased with the results, especially that it had *not* been possible for her as beautiful damsel in distress to complete the role as required: She had felt sorry for Eberhard and had found it unjust that she had to reject him—indeed, she was very near going with him! Only the thought that his nobel renunciation of her was necessary to his further development allowed her to carry through and to disappoint him: "It just had to be." (A personal note: About a year later I ran into the woman again and learned that she had made considerable progress not only in her vocation, but as well in her "femaleness," albeit through both positive and negative experiences.)

Of the two authors, Mr. U had had the basic ideas for this "epic." In the fairy-tale improvisation he played the priest and the blind seer (p. 105, Figures VII and 6), and in *Little Hans* he was Hans' friend who went with him to the soccer field. He had evidently done a great deal of the writing on the script, but "without Mr. R's help and the mutual inspiration I couldn't have done it."

For Mr. R it was very important to show the group, which had continually judged him younger than he actually was, his more mature sides. In the performance of *Frog Prince* (p. 103) he had not been able to make his mark, both in the door scene with the chair and in his jump from the edge of the bed to the feet of the princess. Then the group's youngest member had suggested he play Little Hans, and in the discussion following the performance the others had presumed in him a "desire to remain small." So, the performance of *Philipp and Eberhard* rightly gave him a better position in the group as a whole.

It is possible to see Mr. R's own development throughout the five-day fairy-tale seminar as analogous to that of the hero in a fairy tale. His path had indeed not been an easy one. But together with a "brother" he had finally succeeded in something that was expressed in the development of Philipp and Eberhard.

Meeting in Fairy-Tale Land

If, after weighing the relevant variables of client, therapist, and therapeutic technique, the therapist comes to the conclusion that an even less structured method is required and possible, there are several alternatives available.

- *Metamorphosis*

This form is particularly useful when the group participants are so well acquainted with each other that the initial choosing up of roles is immediately possible and indeed practical. This does not mean, however, that the group must have had experience with other forms of fairy-tale performance beforehand. In individual therapy, a similar suggestion on the fantasy level can comprise the family or all important persons of the past and present, including the client. Thus, we are dealing with a modified form of the "family as animals" with the help of fairy-tale figures (see pp. 25 and 113 on protecting feelings of loyalty). Of course, these images can subsequently be drawn, modeled—or played out. It has proved useful to give the participants the chance before group discussion to imagine for themselves what role from what fairy tale they themselves would like to play, and what roles they think the others might suggest for them. It sometimes helps to advise the participants to close their eyes in order to shut out the group for a while.

When the members have opened their eyes again, I give the instruction that everyone look around in the circle and observe each individual other member very intensely for a while before role selection begins. A further help for the discussion and the later performance is the note that "Everyone must begin the performance in the given role, and he or she can retain this role for as long as desired. But role transformations or metamorphoses are possible at all times." And perhaps one may add: "For this reason we can make role suggestions and role choices relatively freely."

Example:

The following is part of a discussion in a group of patients who were relatively well acquainted with each other; they were all in clinical psychotherapeutic treatment. The attention was presently focused on an approximately 35-year-old woman (Ms. L) who, suffering from various functional disorders, liked to be pampered. And since she was always kind and thankful about it, she regularly found willing helpers. Realization of helpfulness *on her part* was "unfortunately" hindered by her own problems.

Mr. M (who had supported Ms. L several times and comforted her as well): I think Ms. L should get a nice role, she's always so nice and, I would say, somewhat delicate.

Ms. N (who had repeatedly let Mr. M know that she thought him too soft, maybe even unmanly): That's exactly what I would have expected of you!

Ms. O (to Ms. N, with a laugh): Now, now, don't be jealous . . . (Ms. N looks completely surprised and amazed at this comment, as though she can't possibly have been meant) . . . Oh yes, I mean you. Don't think I haven't seen how difficult it is for you to treat yourself to something . . . and so others aren't to get it either.

Ms. N: Are you crazy? She (pointing to Ms. L) can take more than you believe. I would suggest that she really do something for a change, for example, play Goldmarie or Pechmarie, where it becomes clear that ony those who really work and not just act as though they're working are rewarded.

Ms. P: Well, I envisioned her more as the *Princess on a Pea,* way up there on those soft mattresses.

Mr. M: If it has to be a role with work, why not as *Cinderella,* with all those peas and beans. . .

Ms. N (interrupting him): OK, but without the help of the birds!

Mr. R: I think she'd be better as the princess in *King Thrushbeard.*

Ms. O (to Mr. R, somewhat sharply): Why's that? Did she reject you?

Mr. S: Yeah, she has an air of rejection, of pickiness about her.

Mr. M: Well, I don't find Ms. L like that at all. She may be picky, but I see no reason to say "Amen" to everything anyone says.

After a few more minutes of discussion, Ms. L was in fact given the role of princess in *King Thrushbeard*—on the condition that she make her own pottery and sell her own wares. In response to the question what role she would have given herself, Ms. L said the girl in *Sterntaler.* She also noted that the position taken by most of the group reminded her of her parents and brothers and sisters as well as colleagues at work, who regularly spurred her on to strive more—and who did not believe her when she said she couldn't do any more or go any further.

It has proved unfavorable to encourage the participants to back up their suggestions and choices with reasons. However important the aspects mentioned may be, the danger of talking things to death is very present: The working-through phase should be referred to a discussion *after* the performance—though enough time for this purpose must also be set aside.

Role selection can last a long time. While this process is going on, the clients should be reminded that, when choosing a particular figure, they need not consider the fact that other figures will also be present, for example, that there will be dwarfs, a step-mother, *and* a prince in addition to Snow-White.

Before the actual performance begins, the group leader once again should mention the possibility of metamorphoses, adding: "But please try to make it evident, at the very least to yourself, when and under what circumstances you slipped from one role to another. And when changing roles, do not announce the new role—play it! Thus, for example, when the wolf from *Little Red-Riding Hood* experiences a metamorphosis, he should simply stand up, miaul, point proudly to his hat, his jacket, his boots and act courtly—but not call out: "So, now I'm *Puss in Boots!*"

Sometimes the participants, particularly of course in continuing education, want the course leader or therapist to take part in the performance. Nothing generally can be said against the leader or co-leader being issued fitting roles; but otherwise I feel the therapist should rather be the moderator of the discussion surrounding roles, be accepting, and try to turn differences into alternatives. Above all I avoid injecting into the process my own preferences for certain roles or certain clients—however fitting they might be. Suggestions emanating from the therapist not only are taken very seriously (something which can, of course, also be used profitably, at certain junctures), they are easily interpreted as a ranking, grading, or a restriction. For further comments on the therapist's participation, see also my remarks made during the general introduction to fairy-tale performance on pages 66 and 90.

In any case, before I take on a role, and I relatively seldom do, I point out the fact that my function as observer will then be limited: "It's hard for me to really play along if I am to watch the others at the same time and collect impressions. So everyone is going to have to watch out for themselves and register their own impressions so that they can be discussed later." In clinical surroundings, of course, there may be other personnel present who could assume the observer role. In one well-functioning therapeutic community I even had the experience that the patients themselves expressed the wish that the other personnel take over my normal role: They wanted to have the feedback of outsiders on their behavior. In this case the comments of the audience represented a "positive mirroring," unobstructed by feelings of being observed or controlled. Audiovisual means can be of great help here— but only on the condition that the participants are agreed. And even if one gives previous notice of their employment, even if their presence is more or less freely accepted by the participants—a certain portion of the spontaneity is lost. That, as is often said, people "get used to it," is true for the vast majority; but we must also consider those whose participation would be hindered or even blocked by such means. The latter is true especially for insight- or depth-psychology-oriented forms of therapy; in behavior-modifying learning and training therapies, on the other hand, the use of video techniques can have tremendous advantages.

When the group leader assumes a role in a performance, a nearly *parent-free atmosphere* arises. And remember: whatever role the therapist assumes at the beginning, he or she too may take on another form—be metamorphosed.

An example of the metamorphosis of the group leader would be the transformation from being the grocer in *The Wolf and the Seven Kids*, from whom one can *get everything,* to a curious, but bewildered entity from a foreign galaxy. This role change frees the therapist from the wish-fulfillment role desired by the participants—but all under the aegis of foreignness.

As one can easily imagine, out of a slow, difficult, sometimes even boring beginning can arise a very lively, uncontrollable, even chaotic performance. Usually, 10 to 15 minutes suffice to supply an abundance of material for discussion. If a joint action occurs in the group, there should be no objection to having it merge into a (fairy-tale) performance or some other creative method. Usually, however, the one or the other participant becomes tired of playing and withdraws, at which point one should make a "last call." The following alternatives are not meant as recipes, but as examples that may be modified as necessary.

Leader not part of performance

- "Now the time in fairy-tale land is coming to an end."

- "Whoever wants to exit from a role may come to this corner." (where the leader is standing)

- "OK, one more metamorphosis for everyone."

Leader part of performance

- (whispering to the various groups) "Hey, all the fairy-tale figures are gathering over here."

- (in the role of the town crier) "Hear ye, hear ye! All fairy-tale beings to gather in yon magical forest . . ."

Sometimes it suffices as well when the leader and co-leader go to those withdrawing and form a group.

In the discussion phase it is important to pick up on the experiences gained during the performance. Let the participants describe and relate rather than explain, judge, or interpret. Some of the metamorphoses may have to be re-played to those who were busy doing—that is, being—something else. The most important aspect about a metamorphosis is *when* it occurred, what the *differences* are between the two figures, and what the *circumstances* were under which the metamorphosis took place. For the moment, the question f *why* should be put aside, and for good reason: If the matters of how, when, what, and where are discussed thoroughly, the why results as it were automatically. Sometimes it can also be fruitful to learn from the person having experienced the metamorphosis whether he or she "wanted to" or "had to" be transformed, given the circumstances. For example, it is important to know whether the person picked out a favorite role to be metamorphosed into or is rather *fleeing* an intolerable situation. And it should be determined whether the person just had to "get out," or whether he or she was in the position to choose a new and better role.

An example:

Once, while leading a seminar group in continuing education, I was picked for the role of the bear in *Snow-White and Rose-Red,* something I was very agreed to. And since the group not only wanted to have the control, but was also in the position to actually do so, I saw no reason why I should not accept this role. I was doing quite well—even without the two girls: I saved a pigeon from *Puss 'n Boots,* and for this the pigeon showed me the way to a honey tree; I danced with Cinderella, Snow-White, and Goldmarie, all of whom presumed under my matted fur (the inside of a reversible coat) a Prince. Suddenly, however, I realized that they were making a *dancing bear* out of me—missing were only the ring in my nose and the stick. I decided I had to get out of the role somehow. Under a table that served as my cave I took off the fur and wrapped myself in a dark-blue tablecloth so that only my face could be seen. Then I got up onto a chair which I had put up on a stack of school tables; the room had a very high ceiling. There I became the man in the moon—beyond reach and with a good lookout over what was happening below in fairy-tale land.

• Anti-roles and anti-role playing

Schneider-Düker wrote an interesting piece on anti-roles in psychodrama [46]. Even when a story takes place in a fairy-tale world, it contains equally roles that are contrasting and complementary. And both the flexibility of the participants regarding roles and the limits thereof become clear in anti-role-playing. The method of choosing up roles is similar to that described elsewhere in this book (p. 96). It is important, however, that it be decided *beforehand* whether and when role changes are to be allowed. If the participants are free to metamorphose, their natural tendencies toward being ambitious, proficient, and lazy will be decisive in the choice of timepoint. But if the anti-role is to be carried out to the end, the qualities of perseverance and adaptability will be required in addition to that of proficiency. The supernatural world of fairy tales, sagas, and myths should be very broadly defined—and without hard and fast limits—when distributing roles. Whoever is leading such a group must be well acquainted with the individual members, since an anti-role can easily cause feelings of stress and confrontation. In order to act as moderator and catch-all, the therapist needs a strong basis from which to act, and that basis may be found in a certain knowledge of the life history and behavioral characteristics of the participants. In a constructive group and one that respects the peculiarities of the individual, both the choice of anti-roles as well as the anti-role-playing itself offer much relevant material to be studied. Deep insight into one's own personality—one's possibilities and limitations—can be obtained. Even the search for a proper anti-role for oneself can be a mine of revelations. For this reason, I usually allow for more time for this process than, for example, for meeting in fairy-tale land. And I usually make the suggestion that one try to think up not just one, but a number of fitting roles, the best one crystallizing then of its own accord and at the proper time.

An example:

In the same seminar group from which the epic *Philipp and Eberhard* and the free improvisation of fairy tales stem we had the opportunity to put on an "anti-role-play in fairy-tale land." This group, a particularly hard-working one I might add, had nothing against all present taking part: In four days of intensive work together, we had become very well acquainted with each other, and there was no reason to expect that destructive tendencies would gain the upper hand. Here, I would like to report only my own experiences.

The first anti-role that occurred to me was a German female folk hero and figure in a drama by Kleist, which I rejected as not being exactly fairy-tale-like. The second was for the girl from the story of *Sterntaler* whose illusionary expectations would have made for a good contrast; on the other hand, her desire to give others something didn't seem very much of a contrast. Then I thought of the story of *The Thick Porridge*. I had to laugh: The portrayal of sweet, sticky slowness would certainly have been a contrast to my personality, that of thickness certainly not! Suddenly, *Sleeping Beauty* came to me—the 100 years of sleep did not at all fit well with my very lively self. And the very act of being inactive, of waiting on others to appear, gave me an uneasy feeling. However, I then remembered that a great number of princes had remained as skeletons in the thorns—an awful thought perhaps, but evidence enough of the "Sleeping-Beauty narcissism." So I rejected that role, too. The very same moment the next idea occurred to me, and immediately I knew I had found my proper anti-role: the sleeping fly on the wall of Sleeping Beauty's castle—inactive, small, delicate, meaningless (unless as a final sign that truly everything was asleep)!

That I was eventually given another role did not change the truth of my image as the sleeping fly. Finally I was to play the "seductive prima ballerina" of the fairy-tale ballet—despite all my God-given handicaps—and I enjoyed it: I gathered experiences in making seductive overtures, something I would otherwise not allow myself.

The resulting experiences and thoughts may be worked through or used therapeutically either in individual or group sessions, depending on the type of therapy practiced and its goals. Sometimes they form the transitions to other creative activities; see also pages 55, 61, 67, and 96 in this book for discussions of such possibilities, primarily as a transition to verbal working-through.

Free Improvisation of Fairy Tales

This form of fairy-tale performance is completely free in both content and roll make-up. The therapist or group leader should be aware that it can take a long time for things to start rolling—if they roll at all! One often has to sit through a "drought" or two, without intervening or making alternative suggestions. Simply starting a fairy-tale improvisation without carefully choosing the proper point in time will, particularly in a well-motivated group, most probably cause all concerned to be disappointed. Consider especially the expectations and the capabilities of the individual participants as well as of the group as a whole. Leave sufficient time for later verbally working through the experiences. And because this method may cause problems or conflicts to surface in some persons, plan for an intensive follow-up. Also, I usually try to see to it that the free improvisation comes neither at the beginning nor the end of a three- or five-day seminar.

Below is the depiction of one such improvisation, chosen explicitly from a group whose other work I have described elsewhere in this book under invention of fairy tales (p. 36) and performing a tale according to the instructions of the author(s) (p. 90). The experiences of two particular participants (Mr. R and Ms. T) are described in more detail in order that the reader may gain insight into the combined effects of a *series* of work methods involving fairy tales. Some of the (re)actions of the other participants are described as well to illustrate the context.

But first a description of some of the most important experiences of the two above-mentioned participants during the rest of the course.

Mr. R had been suggested to play Hansel, but did not receive enough votes (3rd place). He then played the frog in the second performance of *The Frog Prince*. Three scenes were important for him:

• The well was played by two women who formed the upper edge with their arms. The "frog" crouched down between them, thus seeing nothing of what happened on the meadow (see Figure): He had remained, he later pointed out, "in the deep," just as the story requires. Mr. R's interpretation of the role was the opposite of that in the first performance in which the frog not only looked around at everything, but seemed even to lure the princess. Now, the princess of the second performance had chosen as her golden ball a very agile man (later to play Eberhard, see page 90), who rolled and hopped across the whole room. Mr. R as frog noticed him only when he came rolling into the well and landed on the frog's head. "Ow" the frog said, looked up, and saw the princess. She subsequently had no trouble getting him to fetch the ball; her necessary "promise" was given in passing, as it were.

• The scene in which the frog knocks on the door and seeks entry turned out to be very exciting. The entire court was gathered around the king's table. The frog took a chair (as door), squatted down behind it, and knocked three times loudly on the floor. The conversation at the table stopped. After a few seconds the frog knocked

again. Everyone waited. Then a guest, coming late to the meal, entered from the other side of the room; there being no place left at the table, a lady-in-waiting simply took away the "door," which of course was in fact a chair. Now Mr. R left his role shortly, went and got another chair from the other side of the room, set it up again as the "door," and knocked for the third time. The king, wanting to help, said in a majestic manner: "I thought I heard a knocking . . . but I perceive no voice." Nothing happened. The frog knocked again. At his fifth knocking the king sent the princess to open the door; she could barely hide her embarrassment.

• In the scene in which the frog is supposed to try and get the princess to take him up into her bed, Mr. R was at the foot of the bed and was thus easily pushed off.

In the subsequent discussion of this performance, Mr. R had repeatedly to defend himself against comments that made him seem even slighter than he already felt. He was able to prove on the basis of the original text of the tale that the frog first becomes aware of the princess when he comes out of the deep of the well. The other members of the group had apparently forgotten this, not the least because of the influence tat the performance of the first very active and curious frog had had on them. Likewise, they had expected him to be like the first frog and jump straight into the bed of the princess. Again, Mr. R referred to the text: ". . . lift me up or I'll tell your father." This was accepted—but it was also pointed out that Mr. R had *not* threatened the princess with her father. Where the group did not budge, however, was in its opinion of the scene at the door: Mr. R had not said a thing there.

R: What do you mean? I knocked, didn't I?

Participant (female): Yes you did. But you didn't *say* anything.

King: And I even wanted to help you when I said that no voice could be heard.

R: Yeah . . . well—but (emphatic) I *did* knock!

Participant (male): So what? Why didn't you say: Hey, Princess, sweetie, let me in!

R (restrained, more hurt than angry): But I knocked on the door . . . and when you knock on the door, somebody's first got to say "Come in" or open up.

Reference to the text of the fairy tale was of no avail: Mr. R stuck to his opinion, which of course does correspond to very proper manners. Many in the group thought that this behavior had something to do with Mr. R's own very courteous conduct in the real world. One female participant even thought he had been *too* kind; her feeling was that Mr. R didn't like being judged younger than he actually was. Mr. R confirmed that this was in fact quite often his experience.

Ms. T had lost a very close member of her family a week before the seminar began; she had been the only one present when the sudden death occurred. For the performance of *Hansel and Gretel,* she had chosen the role of the old witch. Later, during the discussion, she said that she thought a lot about death; she had actually intended to delay the death of the witch, to extend that experience. (It was not discussed, I should mention, whether this was meant to be a "conscious death"—unlike that of her relative.) In any case, it was too much for her, so she decided to "die quickly." At another point in the discussion someone mentioned that in that story the evil step-mother dies at the same time as the old witch—almost as though the two were the same person. Maybe the witch wasn't needed any more, a female participant suggested, now that Gretel had become wiser and could "bewitch" herself. The last comment is important and interesting in the sense of "opening up to one's own drk parts." At this juncture, the group took a look at the entire fairy tale on the subject level, viewing all persons, beings, and objects in the tale as parts of the personality of a human being. Gretel would thus be a male's *anima,* his female attributes; for a female, Hansel is a representative of her *animus.* Ms. T took an active part in the discussion, though at this point she had not yet said that she would like to get to know all parts of her own personality better. Of course, no one can really say whether the idea of *dying and becoming* together with the discussion on personality structure actually influenced Ms. T, but it seems a reasonable thought.

The following description of a fairy-tale improvisation is, except for the last part, made from my own standpoint as group leader. At the end, however, I point out some of the passages important for Ms. T, Mr. R, and Mr. U.

The idea of doing a free improvisation of a fairy tale was easily accepted by the group members after they had participated in a few performances and were thus beginning to recognize and formulate their own desires. The weather was good, so we worked outdoors. The group consisted of eight women and six men, including the group leader (myself) and co-therapist (a woman). A slightly hilly meadow at the top of a wooded mountain, known to some of the participants and the leader from earlier trips, served as our "stage." At the northern-most edge, behind and slightly above two very tall trees, stood an oval chapel. The group paused in front of the two trees, and I told the members that from now on there would be no more instructions from either the group leader or the co-therapist—but that we could, of course, as agreed upon, be included in their activities.

At first, everyone just stood around; once in a while two or three persons spoke with each other; but for six or seven minutes basically nothing happened (see Figure 5). The co-therapist looked at me; I shrugged my shoulders. (During the "drought" I did take the opportunity to take a few pictures, though.) In the following two or three minutes there were a few changes in the group make-up: It appeared to me to be an example par excellence of the sociological concept of relations. I wandered past the co-therapist and we agreed to let things go on for a while at least; the burden and responsibility for the group work and for utilizing the limited time available was beginning to weigh heavily on us. Then, shortly thereafter, a very resolute colleague (the same woman who, as lady-in-waiting, had simply removed the frog's "door," as described above) gathered the other women in the group together, and they all went off to the shadows between the trees in front of the chapel. For me at least it was a relief, that something was finally happening.

Then, "we men" gathered; we glanced repeatedly over to the women's group standing some 25 or 30 meters from us. We spoke in short sentences: "I wonder what they're doing" — "It's a conspiracy for sure!" — "They're planning something!" (while we in fact weren't). Then Ms. T began pacing in front of the chapel doorway. Our curiosity grew. We decided that we needed an envoy: one of the group should play a "priest" and go to them—they would surely not harm him. (We had apparently assumed from the gestures of the women that they were planning something against us.) But the chosen colleague (later to play Herrmann refused to play the priest. Next, Mr. U (one of the authors of *Philipp and Eberhard*) was chosen in his stead. He put on a hooded coat, took a "shepherd's staff," and walked slowly and majestically over to the women's group. There a quiet conversation developed (see Figure VII), and only after the "monk" came near the chapel doorway did Ms. T attack him. When he tried to defend himself, the other women took on threatening poses, too. In the group of men mutterings could be heard: "What! They don't even respect a priest!" etc. We decided to attack in order to save our colleague and ran first behind the chapel. I was given the role of messenger who was to enter from one side, panting, totally exhausted, and report that the enemy was coming right after me. (This deception was deemed necessary because of our being in the minority.) Then the other four men would make a surprise attack from the other side; we agreed to take the two most dangerous women as hostages and try to strike a deal with them. Well, we succeeded in surprising them, but that was it: Their resistance was unexpectedly strong, for we men did not yet know that the "cave" (the chapel) contained the *women's treasure,* guarded by the "dragon" (Ms. T). Thus, we had misinterpreted her attack on the priest, as she was only "doing her duty as dragon."

Two of the women were indeed taken captive for a short time. The initiator of the women's group, however, could not be held by the men (who were not very rough, though), and she escaped. My attempt at blocking her path failed. Ms. T hissed like a dragon, but then she stumbled over a colleague's foot and landed flat on her face in the meadow. After a while she stood up; she looked very serene, as though transformed, and said: "Now I am a *woman*." Of course, the men did not understand this statement. They looked puzzled, then one of the women said: "She was a dragon, she was protecting our treasure." From that point on the "battle" lost its interest. A man asked: "What is that, your treasure?" "We don't know either," one woman answered, "but it is very valuable and no one is allowed to see it." Interest in the treasure grew, until I as leader (note the aspects of expectation and transference) was given the duty of looking through the hole in the door (see Figure 6). So I went to the door, looked through the hole, cried "Ahhh," and held my hands in front of my face and called out: "I've been blinded, I can't see anything!" No one paid particular attention to my blindness, rather they all wanted to know *what* I had seen in the moment of being blinded. I answered: "It was totally . . . well . . . totally bright, shining . . . and then I couldn't see any more." Next, the "monk" (Mr. U) was given the task of peering through the hole, in the hope that his position as priest would keep him from being blinded. But when he looked through the hole, he too was blinded and thus became the "blind seer" (Figure 6), who had the ability to "read" or "see" important messages in a mirror with his fingers. For a while he was the center point of an oracle game. (Was Mr. U being animated here already to think up something for the others? Remember that he later wrote part of *Philipp and Eberhard*.)

Later it was unclear who had originally had the idea to encircle the treasure if it weren't possible to discover what it was made of. In any case, the group formed a row, hand in hand, in order to surround the entire chapel. It soon became obvious, however, to our own surprise, that there weren't enough of us to reach all the way round. So everyone pressed themselves against the chapel, our hands touching only at the fingertips, but it still wasn't enough. I myself was not unhappy at this turn—I didn't know why—but I observed a number of very disappointed faces among the group of young men and women. Then it occurred to me: "Of course! Women's treasure, the treasure of a woman—I don't really want to encircle it, to hold onto it, to *capture* it. This treasure should be beyond one's grasp (in both senses of the word). Being together and feeling the other in one's arms suffice." At the same time, however, I realized that 15 years earlier I had thought very differently; I made a note to bring this point up later in the discussion.

The group now gathered behind the chapel, where a very old, somewhat weathered old tree (an official monument, by the way) stood at the edge of the mountainside; there also the forest began. A growth of this tree seemed to be "looking" at us (Figure 7), and it provoked a number of associations: primitive horse . . . moose-father . . . hippopotamus from the deep, etc. (For me it looked like a figure from a story of the Swedish writer Tove Jansson (26)). One participant, who later was to play the chancellor and the black knight, climbed up onto a large, nearly horizontal branch and wanted to play *The Brave Little Tailor*; the wild boars (note: more than one) should run back and forth under the tree and try to reach him. (Perhaps one of the sources for Eberhard's later pigtending?) Ms. T and the man who later played Eberhard were in the meantime trying to "grow" out of the roots of the tree and thus form a "tree sculpture."

Then there was an interlude in which someone said that an enchanted princess in the form of an ant had been caught in the tree and needed to be freed. A number of ants were entering and leaving a slit in the tree; the "saviour" was to be transformed into an ant to get the "princess" out. And who was better fitting than the "Brave Little Tailor"? I helped in his metamorphosis, threw the monk's robe over him, said a magic spell, and pointed to the slit where, as chance would have it, an ant was just going in. "There he is!" one woman called out. Everyone waited with great expectation. I motioned to the co-therapist to get under the robe. And again luck was on our side: Two ants, a small and a large one, came out of the slit together. "There they are!" I said quickly, repeated the magical formula, pulled away the robe (placing myself in front of the slit)—and there they were, the "prince" and "princess." No one had noticed that my co-therapist had hidden herself under the robe. The surprise effect was very large indeed.

In the pause that followed it became known that it was the birthday of the youngest participant in the group. Her first wish could not be fulfilled because we were not acquainted with the text or melody of a song she suggested singing. So she made another suggestion: *Hänschen-Klein* (Little Hans) a popular German children's song with the text:

Little Hans, little man,
roamed alone into all lands.
Staff and hat, that's all he had,
but Little Hans was glad.
Yet the mother cries at home,
now that she has lost her son.
And the child thinks a while,
longs for mother's smile.

We sang it as well as we could, and as birthday present I said she should choose whomever she wanted to play Hans and the mother. For Hans she wanted Mr. R (see above), who moaned: "Oh, not again!" But being his usual friendly self, he added: "But if it's your birthday wish . . ." As mother a particularly warm-hearted woman was chosen. A colleague loaned Mr. R his hat, and a fitting staff was also found. Now everyone returned to the two trees in front of the chapel, where there was more room.

Mr. R took leave of his mother (Figure 8a) and walked (or, rather, he sauntered) into the forest; thus, not really going into the world with burning curiosity, as the song implies. To wake him from his "laid-back," almost absent-minded attitude, I stood in his way, took him by the shoulders, and called out in a rather loud, certain voice: "Ah, yes! A strong young man you are! Now that's the kind of stuff good soldiers are made of!" Mr. R stood there somewhat bewildered. I went on: "Come on, come join us. Be a soldier. If you're brave and if you work hard, you too may become a general one day—like me!" Hans—first somewhat tentatively, then ever stronger— said: "No, no . . . I don't want to." So I let him go and nodded to the co-therapist that she should "meet" him as a young girl. She came from the side and took him by the hand. "Where you going?" she asked in a soft voice. "Oh, I don't really know . . . into the world." "We could walk a while together if you want." To which Hans finally agreed. So the both of them wandered across the meadow.

In the meantime, the mother, completely in the part, was crying for her son, who was now going ever farther away. Someone then suggested: "Why don't you send him a message?" To this another replied by singing the song: "A bird came a' flying / lit down upon my toe / with a note in its beak / your mother says hello." Ms. T was chosen to be the bird, and she took off to chase down Little Hans and the girl. After she'd given him the message, Hans was still not sure what to do. A long debate ensued between the bird and Hans, during which time the mother exclaimed: "Well, now that my son's left, I'll need another man in the house." Everyone laughed, and someone noted: "Oh my, mothers and their sons!" The woman who had started the entire improvisation offered to help the mother look for someone. A very funny scene developed in which she showed the mother how to go about choosing a man— it reminded one somewhat of a livestock auction!

Ms. T in the meantime had become very emphatic and had taken Hans by the hand in order to bring him back home. But the other hand was being held by the girl. Exactly what the circumstances were leading to his following the bird after this tug-of-war could not be made out at such a distance. In any case, the reunion of mother and son was very warm (Figure 8b), warmer in fact than the farewell scene. Yet Hans did not stay with the mother very long, but with the support of Mr. U he took off for the soccer field. This had also been made possible through the mother's telling him that she had found a new lover. (Whether the joint action of Mr. R and Mr. U here led to their later cooperation in writing the epic is not known, but probably not unlikely.)

On this note the improvisation ended—and it was also time to eat lunch, the allotted time having been exceeded by nearly a half an hour. The entire performance, including the first "drought," had lasted about one and one-half hours—to the surprise of nearly all participants. We decided to extend the afternoon session so as to be able to discuss everything extensively.

Now, while writing these words, it appears to me that I have described everything as being much more meaningful than I actually experienced it at that time. While on our way to lunch, I discussed the improvisation shortly with my co-therapist, and we both were not really sure whether the entire performance and the many unrelated scenes and episodes had been of any consequence at all.

The afternoon session was to teach us better. After four and one-half hours (!) of discussion we parted with the feeling that we had, to be sure, mentioned a lot of things, worked through a few things, but that we had certainly not really exhausted the experiental material at hand. Most of the participants wanted to work on their own on the personal aspects of what had occurred.

The description given above includes several thoughts on connections between the improvisation and the group dynamics present during the entire seminar. Thus, I restrict my further comments to a few "waystations" important to the development of Ms. T and Mr. R.

After her experience as the witch in *Hansel and Gretel* (p. 104), Ms. T felt her role as dragon to be very important—not the least because she had simply put her idea "into practice." The aspect of *dying and becoming* (p. 120) was discussed extensively by the group. One (female) colleague saw a connection to the tree sculpture (p. 107) in which Ms. T, as it were, "grew out of her own roots." Ms. T's wish to play not only Rosalind, but also the damsel in distress (p. 91) becomes plausible when seen against the background of her cquainting herself with the various, both subject and object, parts of her personality.

Mr. R also becomes more transparent when one views some of the important events happening during the seminar (and the order in which they occurred). First, he played the (very young) Hansel, then the frog in *The Frog Prince,* so that the suggestion of his playing Little Hans seemed to him to be a repetition—especially as it reminded him of his situation in real life. His way of always being careful and considerate, with tendencies toward adaptation, was opposed in the door scene and even more so in the meeting with the general by his concrete will to go his own way. In the discussion phase, Mr. R mentioned that shortly before the seminar he had served several weeks in the reserve corps, which elicited more than a few knowing grins from the others. His cooperation with another male and the invention as well as the acting-out of the later epic itself were just as important to him as being accepted by the group. Some saw in the warmth of Hans' return home a regression, which may have motivated Mr. R even more to take part in writing the epic. Others, however, interpreted this scene very differently: When together, we experience *difficulties* very intensely; when separated, it is our *longing for each other* that is so poignant.

The "treasure" of the women was discussed from several psychological vantage points: from narcissistic gratification (being that loved, wonderful object), through possessive desires and needs, to claims of recognition and power. It became very clear that loving attention, an equal mixture of agape, fondness, sensuality, eros, and sexuality, can be destroyed or invalidated when these needs are too strong.

Of course, much more was discussed in connection with the improvisation, but space does not permit our relating it all. The background and development of

Mr. U, that of the mother of Little Hans, the chancellor/knight/tailor and many other participants; the theme of mother-son relationship; the oedipal problem; the ability to mature through separation—all these could be elaborated on extensively, as well.

It is not by chance that this presentation of the different ways of working with fairy tales in psychotherapy should end with many unanswered questions. This is, I know, frustrating to anyone desiring a complete treatment. But it is positive by allowing a continuation, by touching on some and presenting other possibilities. And one can only take one step—the next one—anyway. Moreno [40] would, when someone wanted to fit in *all* problems in a single drama, limit the scope and delay some to a later timepoint, saying understandingly: "Oh, that's another psychodrama!" Many fairy tales do the same, by pointing to the future after completion of a particular step involving growth. With these words I would like to end this section on performing fairy tales: ". . . and they lived (experienced, rejoiced, suffered, matured) happily ever after."

Part III:
Advantages of Using Fairy Tales in Psychotherapy

This section concerns the special factors peculiar to the use of fairy tales and other supernatural forms in psychotherapy. It includes as well a discussion of how these peculiarities may be implemented to help the client and to enrich psychotherapeutic possibilities. Through reference to previously mentioned examples, we can limit ourselves to a description of the advantages themselves.

Before touching on the individual aspects involved, however, it should be mentioned that a number of them, in different combinations depending on the experience of the client, are nearly always available. In the examples listed below the factors mentioned are particularly easy to recognize and are of great importance: They were easily "crystalized" and depicted as something "pure." But other aspects may also be simultaneously possible. Thus, I would like to emphasize that the therapist is always confronted with the question of *whether, what, when, how* and *with whom* to mention or to introduce them.

Protection of Feelings of Loyalty and Solidarity

Many clients find it easier to speak about their experiences with fairy tales that played a role in their childhood than to make (evaluative) statements about their relatives. Thus, even in the initial phase of a psychotherapy, it can be advantageous to mention fairy tales and other favorite stories when talking about childhood memories. I have often had the experience that in this way one can enter into a relaxed and informal conversation with the storyteller nearly "automatically," as it were, whereas a detailed questioning on the part of the therapist—no matter how interested and compassionate it may be—intimidates the patient and is felt to be rather like an interrogation. But when patients simply "tell their tales," a common wavelength may be found.

No therapist can know from the beginning whether a question posed (which in his or her opinion simply serves to gain information) will touch a sensitive nerve or cause early resistance. Here, an example:

> The therapist heard from his client that the client's father had been the one to tell bedtime fairy tales; the mother had not been mentioned up to this point. The understandable interest of the therapist led to the question: "And what was your mother doing during this time?" With this the client had to make the choice of either resisting this direction or of recounting the serious conflicts between his parents. Discussion of the client's favorite fairy tale, on the other hand, might have caused less tension and probably would have brought just as much clarity to the therapist. For the client's favorite tale was *Hansel and Gretel*, and he was particularly touched by two passages: the first in which the father resists, albeit only halfheartedly, the mother's suggestion to leave the children behind in the forest; and the second in which the children return to the father at the end of the fairy tale, at which point the patient (and the father, too?) always fantasized all that they could do together with the treasures—without the mother around.

In later stages of therapy it can be facilitative when working through particularly painful experiences of the client with his or her important persons—whom one always loves and needs—to remain on the fantasy level. Thinking up a fairy-tale-like story hurts feelings of loyalty a lot less than a direct "betrayal" of family secrets, regardless of how carefully this is carried out.

For other questions and examples concerning loyalty, solidarity, and integrity, see pages 25, 67, and 96.

The General Character of Fairy Tales

As mentioned in the "Preface," this aspect helps clients to get rid of the feeling of being alone in the world with their problems. Many patients—and particularly depressives, who tend to locate all mistakes and the entire "guilt" in their own persons—feel that because of their fears, compulsions, functional disorders, and psychosomatic illnesses they are something separate, apart, deviant, excluded. And one should not forget the equally important narcissistic injury usually present, which is of varying intensity, depending on the individual personality as well as the extent of the formation of an ego-ideal.

The actions and reactions resulting from the experience of being the *only* person affected, the *only* incapable, the *only* inferior person around, may be mitigated by the universality of certain fairy tales. They are certainly more effective than direct, however well-meant expressions of "understanding," which are often interpreted as simple consolation, especially by depressives. One prerequisite, however, to fairy tales playing a helpful role in this sense is that the patient does not consider, and thus reject, all supernatural things as being nothing but craziness, nonsense, or childish old-wives tales. But at the right time in persons receptive to them, fairy tales can, in their simple and clear language, not only show that one has understood, they can also give impulses to dealing constructively to overcome the problems or the life situation at hand.

An example:

Following the accidental death of their six-year-old son, a family lived a life of pain and sorrow; they were unable to enjoy anything, "now that he is no longer with us." Even the four-year-old daughter appeared dejected and passive. In the course of conversations with the parents, it turned out that the earlier evening readings of fairy tales had ceased, and so I picked up on the tradition: I read the Brothers Grimm tale of the *Death Shroud* slowly and clearly, changing only one passage by adding quietly to the sentence ". . . otherwise I cannot fall asleep in my coffin . . ." the words ". . . and my sister cannot live on." The parents looked at each other, clearly moved; the relatively young mother soon began to cry, her husband held her hand in his. I was silent. After a few minutes, the woman sat up, wiped away her tears, blew her nose quite audibly, looked squarely at her husband, and said: "It's true, we must do something . . . it's no better for him (the dead child) if we are all dead."

One female client who had tried to deal with her problems alone and suffered from great anxieties felt lonely and lost; it was a relief for her to discover that many young people throughout time must have experienced such loneliness for it to be so distinctly anchored in fairy-tale figures.

Even the fact alone that clients have to admit to their own need for therapy of their psychological disorders (whatever they may be) is a more or less painful narcissistic injury. Thus, it is all the more important not to increase this injury, especially to the point where therapy itself is no longer possible. We are all liable to injury in our primary and, in my opinion, principally positive narcissistic needs. For this reason, one must treat members of training groups and continuing education courses equally gently as patients who seek out a psychotherapist because of particular problems. The universality of the fairy tale is, of course, a help only when dealing with that part of the injury that says "I am the only (incapable, deviant, disturbed, etc.) person around." Further help may be found in the identification with the fairy-tale hero or another fairy-tale figure (cf. pp. 2, 17, and below).

If there is the danger that the actions of one participant might evoke a narcissistic injury in another participant in the group situation, the therapist should intervene—for both sides' sake—in a moderating and, if possible, positive way. This may be seen, for example, in the therapist's suggestion during the discussion phase of *The Wolf and the Seven Kids* (p. 74), after it had become apparent that some of the participants were primarily interested in criticizing the others.

Concerning avoiding narcissistic injury, I have made some comments in connection with anti-role-playing (p. 100), which actually *furthers* confrontation through its high level of freedom. But then we are dealing mainly with literary and personal fairy tales, where the universality is dependent upon how strongly and intensively basic human feelings are present in such personal visions. Nevertheless, I believe that some of the examples of personal fairy tales and group creations given in this book may indeed reach many persons, though certainly not all. And don't forget that a certain narcissistic pleasure, besides the pleasure found in simply being creative and productive, is offered by the modification of well-known fairy tales—and even more so by the creation and structuring of one's own fairy-tale stories. This may be seen in various examples discussed, but especially in *Philipp and Eberhard* (pp. 36 and 58).

Fosters a Positive Approach to Encountering Conflicts and Problems

In most well-known fairy tales the question of *whether* one should or should not take up something new—a difficulty, a conflict, etc.—arises only marginally. Rather, obstacles are often described that lead to growth or failure. This readiness to take on matters, and the experience that development is hardly possible without risks, dangers, and tests, can help clients in their therapy. And in fairy tales often the naive approach, the happy-go-lucky manner, or even disobedience, is rewarded. In any case, it becomes obvious that sham solutions or acting "as if" definitely does not lead to the goal, namely, maturation: personal growth. This may be observed quite clearly in the tale of *Frau Holle* in the figures of Gold-marie and Pechmarie.

In the examples given in this book of personal fairy tales , the aspects of initiative and activity may be found especially in the Prince of the *Elf Queen* (pp. 12 and 93) as well as in *Philipp and Eberhard* (pp. 36 and 58). The experience of Ms. T (p. 94) and Mr. R (p. 95) show as well the advantages of working on and through the situation on the fairy-tale level.

Identification with the Fairy-Tale Heroes and Other Figures

The aspects mentioned here, of course, quite often interact. If a figure from a fairy tale has suffered similarly and has had to face at least somewhat similar vicissitudes, then "I am not alone" (p. 14). And my relatives are special only in the particular way in which they influence *me*—but they are not the first and certainly not the only ones who have had such effects or who have tried to stop (to them) frightening or disturbing developments.

A well-thought-out distribution of roles in the performance of fairy tales (cf. p. 68) allows the client to test behavioral and (re)action modes not previously available. At the beginning of a therapy, it is usually wise to start the person on a "supporting role" (pp. 67 and 69). Watch for signs in the respective persons which point the way to the proper roles. Admiration of a particular figure or an event in a story—often exhibited only as a short flash in the eyes or an apparent interest—or timid introduction of certain turns in the plot and tendencies of the characters during fairy-tale invention, often suffices as hint. But when fascination becomes overtly evident, one cannot simply oversee it; on the other hand, one should not try to force a "realization" thereof—even on the theatrical or playful level: Breaking new ground is something that has to be discovered and worked at if it is to be a fruitful venture.

The well-known traditional fairy tales and the figures appearing therein are particularly well suited for pointed use in psychotherapy. This is true both for reading and reciting as well as for drawing, painting, or acting out tales and scenes. I would suggest that the interested reader test both traditional fairy tales and personal or newly invented ones for their suitability. For example, one could ask: "Which wishes or signs of identification can I assume or discover in my clients when viewing a certain fairy-tale figure?" or "Which characteristics or capabilities may be stimulated, worked through, or reinforced through identification with a particular figure or event?" Sometimes matters of drive and impetus are at the forefront, sometimes relationships and conflicts.

For example, if a difficult sibling relationship is present, one could suggest, among others, the seven dwarfs in *Snow-White* or *Cinderella* and her step-sisters. The story of *The Wolf and the Seven Kids* has been discussed in detail (p. 68) in this respect. In the example of *Sleeping Beauty* (p. 61), on the other hand, the participant showed strong tendencies toward independence—but not without reason: The text of the fairy tale clearly says that Sleeping Beauty was alone in the castle on her 15th birthday, and that she went looking around on her own.

A patient once said during a group session, with great reproach: "My parents failed to make me independent," to which another participant reacted: "Do you really believe that you can become independent because of something your parents do for you? The hero of *The One who Left to Learn to Fear* would never have gotten to know terror had he sat at home the whole time." The patient then did in fact play the main part in a performance of this fairy tale, and apparently neither of them noticed that the remark may have been exactly the nudge the patient had never received from his parents.

With self-authored tales, identification is common not only on the part of the author, but also of all participants. If, for example, we view the path Ms. T and Mr. R took throughout the entire fairy-tale seminar (pp. 36, 90, and 103) under the aspect of identification, we discover that traditional and newer fairy tales were equally valuable. In fact, each fairy tale has some special aspect that lends itself to identification.

Experiences in the Border Realms Between the Real and the Fairy-Tale World

The transitions between the real world and the fairy-tale world have been shown and delineated for various fairy tales more or less clearly (e.g., pp. —, —). However, it is not only a matter of who in the fairy tale itself can make that crossing and participates on the other side (Goldmarie–Pechmarie); also when reading, reciting, painting, drawing, or acting out tales not all persons can equally accept the fantasy aspect, some not even the allegorical aspect—not to speak of actually entering into and taking part in this world. With this comment I do not mean to criticize such people; rather, I would like to show the importance of this circumstance, that it can hinder both life and therapy.

The border realms offer in any case the possibility of strong emotional involvement. In addition to the dramatic aspects and the conflicts found in the basic situation, there is something unknown present, something puzzling, something fascinating, containing both risks and chances. Being touched and moved by such matters means true emotional involvement—an important piece of information for the therapist. For this reason I have emphasized particularly the small signs of transition from the real to the fairy-tale world (and vice versa); see, for example, pages 50 and 65. In a group situation and for certain individuals as well, however, sometimes a participant's *not* entering the fantasy world can actually be positive and lead to such involvement (p. 76), which may in the end be of help to the person in question. For as soon as emotional involvement is present at all, the path is free for deep and promising developments in the fairy-tale world.

Meeting with Representatives of Supernatural Beings and Archetypes

Every meeting between fairy-tale heroes and beings or forces with supernatural capabilities or characteristics should be viewed from various angles, at the very least on the subject and object level. The object level gives us information on the relationships with and to past or present important persons; the subject level reveals the intrapsychic forces at work. However, I would like particularly to warn against mixing the two: The very realistic and great danger is then present that the therapist, depending on his or her own inner structure, will find positive or negative signs—without noticing that he or she may have actually "planted" them in the client.

An example:

A female patient's declared favorite fairy tale was *The Goose Girl*; the dead, good-hearted mother of the princess reminded her of her own, in the meantime rather idealized mother, and she associated Falada and the understanding king with her own father. She saw in the "evil maiden" her own egoistic tendencies as well as her desires for power and respect, which, she said, all too easily overcame her good, but weak positive characteristics. And because he was so weak and bad, she thought she was dependent on the help and support of other, stronger and better individuals. When she mentioned all this during a group session following a fairy-tale performance, one of her co-patients expressed surprise: She had seen in the maiden her own sister, but had been reminded by Conrad that she had always enjoyed combing her own mother's hair. For her Conrad's fascination with the golden hair of the princess contained characteristics of her own personality. Thus, the same tale was interpreted both as proof of one's own failings and as an example of how I can be good and my sister evil.

If the meeting with supernatural forces and figures causes reactions of intense emotional involvement and feeling, it is usually wise to study the entire scene, the fairy tale, or the particular incident at hand on the one and then on the other level. Choose the aspect that is closest to the experience of the client. All possible interpretations are valid only on an individual basis, and thus are to be used and judged only in connection with the life history and life situation as well as the personality structure of the respective client. One's own—in itself very valuable—knowledge of symbols, archetypes, myths, and magical and supernatural beings forms for therapeutic work the general, broad background against which the uniqueness of individual experience becomes all the more clear.

I never fail to be surprised by the experience of how confrontation with fairy-tale material leads to such strong inner involvement, and how inner forces are set free at such moments. Again, I would like to remind the reader of the importance of small and seemingly inconsequential details (pp. 50, 65).

A final word on the necessary care a therapist must take when working with supernatural, archetypical figures. Such beings affect the deepest, unconscious realms of the person involved, and they therefore sometimes lead to feelings and convictions for which there are often no logical reasons. This inner security then can lure one to make projection about the future. In such cases it is better to say little and avoid "prophetic" statements.

An example:

During a 6-day seminar in continuing education, a very lively, usually happy, and extroverted female participant had repeatedly been judged by others as being 22–23 years of age, although she was in fact already 30. In the performance of *The Shoes that Were Danced to Pieces,* she played one of the 12 princesses (though we actually only had three pairs). As chance would have it, her (prince) partner was a very sensitive, deeply emotional colleague. During the boat trip and while dancing, they both were overcome by an "enchanted fairy-tale mood." Later, during the discussion, they continued to sit, very still, next to each other; and when it came time to act out another story, *Sleeping Beauty,* the woman was—not surprisingly—chosen to play the main part. She begged off, saying that she was still too moved by the last performance. One could see in her face that this was the truth, so another person was chosen. Even during the evening get-together she was somehow "different," quieter and less lively than usual: She looked as though she were very absorbed with herself.

The following day was the last day of the seminar, and the woman seemed to me to be a little too bubbly during the final session. She gave the (very warm-hearted) co-leader a kiss and called her "moms." But when she wanted to say good-bye to me in the same exaggerated manner, I stopped her and said: "Oh, not that way, please," adding with an even voice: "I rather could imagine that after your experience in the performance, you won't be satisfied any longer with pure gaiety. But I do very much hope that you can have both." Even though I had expressed myself very mildly and carefully, more so in fact than I actually felt, I later was uncertain. How, I asked myself, could I be so sure of myself of having seen things correctly? To be sure, a few points supported my position, though they were not completely convincing. And what gave me the right in the first place to offer this person such (unrequested) advice, no matter how carefully I had phrased it? The truth was no permission had been granted and I had no right. Rather, I had only had the experience of her being touched and was convinced that what I had said was "correct": It was my sincere desire that the aspects emerging in her during the performance might develop further. My own "freedom of speech" in that situation continued to concern me greatly, and all the greater was my relief and joy a year or so later when I ran into the woman again, who in the meantime had experienced both difficult and good things and had, in my opinion, become both a very sensitive *and* a happy person.

Promotes Metamorphic Phenomena

During and through meetings with fairy-tale beings transformations become possible. In the transition between the real and the fairy-tale world (pp. 76, 118), metamorphoses and enchantments occur, for example, the petrifaction of *Jorin-gel* in front of the castle wall, the blinding of the Prince in the rose thicket in *Rapunzel,* and the transformation into a fawn in *Little Brother and Sister.* This type of metamorphosis may also be seen as a testing or as support on the road to growth, maturation, and individuation. Such events are less a complete transformation with all previous characteristics being subtracted, as the *addition* of capabilities and functions, requiring that only a few old characteristics be sacrificed.

In a psychotherapy that promotes insight, it is the extent of the new structures which is decisive. Relapses and breakdowns tend to be greater after radical changes than with "small steps," which are easier to integrate into the existing personality. The question then arises when and under what circumstances the newly won capabilities should come to be exercised—and when the "old" behavioral patterns and habits are better suited. Part of and necessary to any true metamorphosis is the *death* of the one, the known part, and the *becoming* of the new. It is as though one were chewing the old and mixing it with the new to ease digestion, leading to a new development, an individual creation.

Many of the examples given in this book concern metamorphic phenomena (pp. 48, 76, 97, and 99) up to and including the all-encompassing one of dying and becoming.

The paths taken by fairy-tale heroes and other supernatural figures as well as by the reader, storyteller, and fairy-tale writer through magical worlds are great adjuncts in psychotherapy. Again: Not everything old must die so that something new can arise in its place! Rather, we should be reminded of a thought of Goethe: "What you inherit from your forebears" (what you bring along and are born with), "acquire in order to possess" (to use it and live it in accordance with one's personality).

References and Sources

1. Andersen, H. C.: Märchen. Frankfurt a.M., Insel Taschenbuch, IT 133, Bd. I–III, 1976.
2. Bettelheim, B.: The Uses of Enchantment. The Meaning and Importance of Fairy Tales. New York, Knopf, 1976.
3. Busch, D.: Märchen. Skizzen einfühlender Deutungen als analytische Lehrstücke der Kindheits- und Jugendpsychologie. Heidelberg, Eigenverlag, Fachbuchhandlung K. Scholl.
4. Clauser, G.: Märchen als Rollenspiel. In: Arzt im Raum des Erlebens. München 1959.
5. Crames, C.: Das Märchen in der Psychiatrie. Inaugural Dissertation. Eberhard Karls-Universität, Tübingen 1975.
6. Dieckmann, H.: Das Lieblingsmärchen der Kindheit und seine Beziehung zur Neurose und Persönlichkeitsstruktur. Praxis d. Kinderpsychologie und -psychiatrie, Heft 6, Aug./Sept. 1967.
7. Dieckmann, H.: Märchen und Traum als Helfer des Menschen. Stuttgart, Bonz, 1968.
8. Drewermann, E., Neuhaus, I.: Der goldene Vogel. Grimms Märchen tiefenpsychologisch gedeutet. Olten, Walter, 1982.
9. Franz, M.-L.: Das Problem des Bösen im Märchen. In: Studien aus dem C. G. Jung Institut, XIII: Das Böse. Zürich, Rascher, 1961.
10. Franzke, E.: Das Psychodrama als gestaltungstherapeutisches Verfahren in einer analytisch orientierten psychosomatischen Klinik. In: Petzold, H. (Hrsg.): Angewandtes Psychodrama in Therapie, Pädagogik, Theater und Wirtschaft. Paderborn, Junfermann, 1972.
11. Franzke, E.: Der Mensch und sein Gestaltungserleben. Bern, Huber, 1977.
12. Freud, S.: Die Traumdeutung. Frankfurt/M., Fischer Bücherei, 428/429, 1964.
13. Freud, S.: Märchenstoffe in Träumen. Ges. Werke, Bd. X. Frankfurt/M, S. Fischer, 1967.
14. Freud, S.: Das Motiv der Kästchenwahl. Ges. Werke, Bd. X, Frankfurt/M., S. Fischer, 1967.
15. Freud, S.: Erinnern, Wiederholen, Durcharbeiten. Ges. Werke, Bd. X, Frankfurt/M., S. Fischer, 1967.
16. Freud, S.: Jenseits des Lustprinzips. Ges. Werke, Bd. XIII. Frankfurt/M., S. Fischer, 1963.
17. Fromm, E.: The Lost Language. New York, Holt, Reinhart and Winston, 1951.
18. Gräser, L.: Die Familie in Tieren. München/Basel, Reinhardt, 1957.
19. Grimm, J., Grimm, W.: Kinder- und Hausmärchen. Gesammelt durch die Brüder Grimm. Frankfurt/M., Insel Taschenbuch, IT 112–114, 1976.
20. Guerin, A.: Psychodrama und Familientherapie unter besonderer Berücksichtigung der Loyalität des Indexpatienten. Überlingen, Moreno- Institut, 1983.

21. Harding, G.: Leken som avslöjar. Stockholm, Natur och Kultur, 1965.
22. Heyer, G. R.: Organismus der Seele. München, J. F. Lehmann, 1959.
23. Högberg, Å.: Symboler, Sagor, Metaforer. Stockholm, Wahlström o. Widstrand, 1984.
24. Hoffmann, H.: Der Struwwelpeter. Bayreuth, Loewes Verlag.
25. Horetzky, O.: Das gezielte Pantomimenspiel in der Gruppenpsychotherapie. Topic Probl. Psychoth. 4, Basel/New York, Karger, 1963.
26. Jansson, T.: Det osynliga barnet. Helsingfors, Gebers, 1969.
27. Jung, C. G.: Praxis der Psychotherapie. Ges. Werke, Bd. 16. Zürich, Rascher, 1958.
28. Kast, V.: Wege aus Angst und Symbiose. Olten, Walter, 1982.
29. Kast, V.: Mann und Frau im Märchen. Olten, Walter, 1983.
30. Kast, V.: Paare. Stuttgart, Kreuz Verlag, 1984.
31. Kemper, W.: Der Traum und seine Be-Deutung. rororo (rde) 4. Reinbek, Rowohlt.
32. Knobloch, F., Knobloch, J.: Integrated Psychotherapy. New York, Jason Aronson, 1979.
33. Kyber, M.: Gesammelte Märchen. Hamburg, C. Wegner, 1949.
34. Kyber, M.: Tiergeschichten. Hamburg, C. Wegner, 1951.
35. Leuner, H. C.: Katathymes Bilderleben. Grundstufe. Stuttgart, Thieme, 1981.
36. Leutz, G. A.: Das klassische Psychodrama nach J. L. Moreno. Berlin, Springer, 1974.
37. Lindgren, A.: Pippi Langstrumpf. Hamburg, Oetinger, 1971.
38. Maaß, H.: Theorie und Praxis der Gestaltungstherapie in der psychosomatischen Klinik. In: Beiträge zur Inneren Medizin. Stuttgart, Schattauer, 1964.
39. Moreno, J. L.: Gruppenpsychotherapie und Psychodrama. Stuttgart, Thieme, 1959.
40. Moreno, J. L.: persönliche Mitteilung, Psychodramakongreß, Wien/Baden 1968.
41. Nell, R.: persönliche Mitteilung, Lindauer Psychotherapiewochen 1975.
42. Petzold, H. (Hrsg.): Angewandtes Psychodrama in Therapie, Pädagogik, Theater und Wirtschaft. Paderborn, Junfermann, 1972.
43. Petzold, H.: Masken und Märchenspiel als Verfahren in der integrativen Therapie. In: Petzold, H. (Hrsg.): Dramatische Therapie. Stuttgart, Hippokrates, 1982.
44. Riemann, F.: Grundformen der Angst. München/Basel, Reinhardt, 1961.
45. Riemann, F.: Die Struktur des Analytikers und ihr Einfluß auf den Behandlungsverlauf. In: Fortschritte der Psychoanalyse I. Göttingen 1964.
46. Schneider-Düker, M.: Zur diagnostischen und therapeutischen Bedeutung der Übung "Gegenrollen finden und spielen" in einer Psychodramagruppe. Abschlußarbeit. Überlingen, Moreno-Institut, 1983.
47. Schultz-Hencke, H.: Lehrbuch der analytischen Psychotherapie. Stuttgart, Thieme, 1951.
48. Schultz-Hencke, H.: Lehrbuch der Traumanalyse. Stuttgart, Thieme, 1961.
49. Swahn, J.-Ö.: Trollen. Stockholm, Bonnierfakta, 1984.
50. Wittgenstein, O. v.: Märchen, Träume, Schicksale. Fischer Taschenbuch, Geist und Psyche 42114, Frankfurt a.M., S. Fischer, 1981.

Subject Index